# ANIMATED
# STORYTELLING

## SIMPLE STEPS FOR CREATING
## ANIMATION & MOTION GRAPHICS

### LIZ BLAZER

**Animated Storytelling**
Simple Steps for Creating Animation & Motion Graphics
**Liz Blazer**

Peachpit Press

Find us on the Web at www.peachpit.com.
Peachpit is a division of Pearson Education.
To report errors, please send a note to errata@peachpit.com.

Acquisitions Editor: Nikki Echler McDonald
Production Editor: Tracey Croom
Development Editor: Jan Seymour
Copy Editor: Jan Seymour
Proofreader: Kim Wimpsett
Compositor: Kim Scott, Bumpy Design
Indexer: James Minkin
Front Cover Design: Ariel Costa
Cover Illustration: Ariel Costa
Back Cover Design: Laura Menza
Interior Design: Laura Menza

ISBN 13: 9780134133652
ISBN 10: 013413365X

9 8 7 6 5 4 3 2 1

Printed and bound in the United States of America

**This book is dedicated to:**

Evan Story Oliver and Jeff Oliver

**Acknowledgments:**

Arial Costa, for sharing his spirit, immense talent, and artistry. His illustrations on the cover and throughout this book are the work of a multitalented wizard.

Nikki McDonald, for supporting this book in every way. It has been an honor and privilege to work with you.

Jan Seymour, the editor every writer hopes for—supportive, sharp as a whip, and creative. Jan, you made the editing process free of stress and full of joy.

To the Peachpit crew, Tracey Croom, Mimi Heft, Kim Scott, and Kim Wimpsett, thank you for your care and professionalism in helping me complete this book.

I humbly thank and am deeply indebted to Robin Landa, Christine Panushka, Denise Anderson, Laura Menza, Marc Golden, Bill Moore, Brian Oakes, Brooke Keesling, Alan Robbins, Karin Fong, Kim Dulaney, Sterling Sheehy, Greg Araya, Colin Elliot, Erin Elliot, Mike Enright, Yoriko Murakami, USC School of Cinematic Arts, TED Active, TED-Ed, Stephanie Lo, Jeremiah Dickey, Sarah Shewey, Kelly Young Stoetzel, Elizabeth Daley, Kathy Smith, Sheila Sofian, Lisa Mann, Mar Elepano, John Andrews, Leah Shore, Elaine Montoya, Becky Padilla, Justin Cone, Carlos El Asmar, Ron Diamond, Bonita Blazer, Jon Blazer, and Sheldon Blazer.

This book could not have been written without the collaboration, editing, and love from my husband, Jeff Oliver.

**Art Credits:**

Ariel Costa, Cody Walzel, Sirirat Yoom Thawilvejakul, Phil Borst, Jamie Caliri, Louis Morton, Michael Waldron, Richard Borge, Sterling Sheehy, Colin Elliot, Nathalie Rodriguez, Jiali Ma, Kim Dulaney, Passion Pictures, Psyop, The Mill, Von Glitschka, Ian Wright, Jordan Bruner, Maciek Janicki, Gregory Herman, Stefan Bucher, Hsinping Pan, James Lancett, Sean Weston, An Ngo, Richard E. Cytowic, TED-Ed, Alberto Scirocco, leftchannel, Karin Fong, Sony PlayStation, Imaginary Forces, Miguel Jiron, Marsha Kinder, Mark Jonathan Harris, Scott Mahoy, and Julia Pott

## Table of Contents

# INTRODUCTION

We live in a magical era for animated storytelling. Film festivals have sprung up worldwide to celebrate new animation, television and the web are packed with animated content for both kids and adults, and advertisers are hungrily seeking fresh talent to connect with audiences in a meaningful way. Skilled storytellers specializing in animation are in high demand, and the opportunities to thrive in the field are ever expanding. And yet (until now) it has been difficult to find a resource aimed at providing the skills necessary to become a successful animated storyteller.

This book is a step-by-step guide on how to make great stories for both animation and motion graphics. It's based on the idea that whether you are creating a character-based narrative or experimental film for festivals, an advertisement for television or the web, or a motion graphics title sequence, being intentional about storytelling is the key to success.

In ten simple steps beginning with pre-production and storyboarding through color and sound and finally to animation, this book will provide you with the tools you need to create an effective animated story. You'll find concise explanations, useful examples, and short assignments allowing you to set the theory you've learned into action. You'll also find hints on how to take full advantage of animation's limitless potential.

Big consideration went into the idea of exploring animation alongside motion graphics in the same book. The two forms are often treated as if they come from different worlds. Certainly, they grew up in different neighborhoods. Animation (for the most part) has been lumped into the filmmaking discipline, with its commitment to experimental and character-driven stories destined for television, movie theaters, and video game consoles. The study of motion graphics, meanwhile, has been part of the graphic design discipline, where its focus on branding and content promotion has made it essential to advertisements, broadcast graphics, and film titles, to name a few. Animation and motion graphics have been kept apart, and yet these two forms have much in common and so very much to learn from one another. They are presented together in this book because they exist hand-in-hand and because their lessons are mutually beneficial.

For you animated filmmakers eager to get your experimental short into the Ottawa International Animation Festival, you'll find plenty in this book that speaks directly to your goal, but I also urge you to be influenced by the "commercial" culture of motion graphics which stresses discipline and strict deadlines. It will help you get that short completed and mailed off to Canada in time. And for you motion graphics artists working on a new commercial spot, I address you directly and often, but pay close attention to the lessons of animation's experimentalism and storytelling structures. Your motion work will thrive under its influence.

So flip a page and start the fun. Get ready to learn scores of practical skills, but know you're also headed on a personal journey. This is about you gaining the confidence to tell the stories you've always wanted to tell and becoming the storyteller you were always meant to be. Let's get to it... *and may the animated storytelling begin!*

# 1

# PRE-PRODUCTION
## The doorway to a well-planned animated piece

Animation is a limitless storytelling medium. Artists can create worlds, defy gravity, flip from factual to fantasy, and transport audiences to places they never imagined. But jumping right into animation before completing the stages of pre-production is kind of like climbing into the ring with a prizefighter without having had a single boxing lesson. You might get a lucky jab in here or there, but after that it's going to be a bloodbath.

Animated storytelling is all about planning. Most failed projects reach that low point because a director began animating before answering three essential questions about the project: *What is it? What does it look like?* and *What is it made of?* In this chapter you'll answer these questions in three simple steps: Concept Development, Previsualization, and Asset Building.

If you learn nothing else from this entire book, learn that *the animation muse* is secretly an anxious planner and you must learn from her example. When she comes to visit, she expects her guest room to be tidy with a detailed itinerary of all the places you're going to take her laid out on her bed, maybe even some mint chocolates on the pillow. Set up the muse's guest room as she likes; in other words, take pre-production very seriously or risk wasting weeks, even months, working on scenes that don't fit or, worse, fail to complete your project. Ignore these steps at your own peril!

# CONCEPT DEVELOPMENT
## *What is it?*

The single most annoying question you can ask an artist: "So, what's your piece about?" The most prevalent response: "Um, I'm not ready to talk about it." Well, get ready to talk about it, Picasso. Clarity is king in *concept development*, whether you're making a visually driven animated festival film or a client-commissioned motion graphics piece with either "something to tell" (such as a public service announcement) or "something to sell" (like an advertisement). Until you can answer the nagging question of what exactly it is you're doing, go no further.

## Start with a Creative Brief

If you're working with a client, whether it be on a high-budget film trailer, a public service announcement (PSA) for a website, or an advertisement for TV, you'll most likely be given a *creative brief*. If done right, this document should explain the client's aims and objectives (what the project must be and how long), audience, and milestone deadlines for the project. Corporate culture doesn't always get it right, but they're onto something here. The creative brief forces the client and creative to get on the same page (or at least somewhere close). If you're not working with a client, then I highly recommend that you write your own creative brief.

We all have our eccentric processes and nothing's sure-fire. But I like to step away from the computer, tape a bunch of blank pieces of paper to the wall, and break out a Magic Marker. What? You don't have any paper? OK then, Post-it Notes®? They'll do fine! Just step away from the computer, grab some kind of writing utensil, and write down the following basic information:

***What must it be?*** Short film, PSA, advertisement, movie trailer, etc.

***Who is it for?*** Film festivals, TV audience consisting of 11- to 14-year-old boys, my aunt Maureen, etc.

***How long must it be?*** Thirty seconds, two minutes, etc.

***What is your objective with the piece?*** To sell diapers, to raise money for breast cancer, to introduce a complex world in a feature film, etc.

***When is it due?*** In a month, in six months, etc.

# THE CREATIVE BRIEF

I highly recommend creating a calendar that works backwards from the absolute due date with weekly milestones that you intend to stick to along the way. Simply Google "blank calendar," print that baby out, and mark a milestone on each Saturday that *must* be met or you don't get to go to Sam's 90s bash on Saturday night.

Done? Good. Answering the previous questions is like tidying up for the muse, which is smart, because she's nearly arriving for her first visit.

## Summon the Muse

You now know *what your project must be, who it's for*, and *when the milestones are due*, but you still don't know what your project *is*. Again, step away from your computer; the muse will pop in to help when you're active and brainstorming. Now, approach the blank pages or Post-its® that you've taped to the wall and write your *Big Idea* up at the top. For a personal project that Big Idea is up to you; perhaps you want to create a short film inspired by a recent break-up and your Big Idea to explore is *first love*. With a client-based assignment you'll likely be given the Big Idea, for example, a PSA on water pollution or an airline commercial about bringing family together. Now grab that marker tight, because here goes!

I want you to write down *everything* you know and feel about your Big Idea, whether it's first love or the airline commercial. Completely empty your brain of your associations with that Big Idea onto the pages.

With first love, explore the memories, wonders, pain, images that flash in your mind, words that you associate with it no matter how bizarre, and so on. For an advertisement for an airline, write down recollections of past flights and imagery and emotional connections you have to travel. Don't worry if it's negative (bad airline food or the size of the bathroom) because you can always flip that later. The point is, total honesty. Write those things down, filling as many pages as you can until you have nothing left to write—literally until your head is completely empty of anything else to say on the subject.

Once you've released all thoughts and free associations on the subject, push yourself to write down two or three more things. This whole process should take between 15 and 30 minutes.

# THE BIG IDEA

### The story is up there!

Now that you've emptied your brain on the subject of your Big Idea, circle the words and ideas that you find most compelling. Try to narrow the list to your favorites—maybe four or five great ones. Sometimes there will be a nice connection between the best ones. If it's first love that you've explored, then you might circle an idea like "It's about accepting faults" or an image like "The way his shoelaces were always untied." The subject of airline travel might offer images of being greeted by a loved one at the airport, the word "takeoff," or even cramped space in coach and the dream of one day having more legroom and a soft cushion in first class.

Storytelling is as old as dirt. People have been making up stories since cave dwelling times. Our brains are wired to make connections and find narratives. Yes, your brain, too.

For your story of first love, for instance, just focusing on the feeling that love is "about accepting faults" and the images of "his untied shoelaces" may spark a narrative in your mind. Just riffing here, but let's say it's about a neat and prim girl who loves a very messy boy whose shoelaces are always untied. She keeps trying to neaten the messy boy up and always ties his shoelaces even though he prefers them untied. They get in a fight over it and break up. The neat girl is inconsolable—she misses the boy and even his sloppy, untied shoes. She runs out to find him but there he is at her door. He has flowers and is dressed very tidily with his shoelaces all laced up. The girl smiles seeing that he changed for her. She takes the flowers but then bends down and unties his shoes and musses up his hair. The boy smiles widely, seeing that she finally loves him for who he is.

For the airplane ad we identified "takeoff" and being cramped in coach and dreaming of sitting in first class with more legroom and a soft pillow. So, maybe we start with that image of a person (Jane) stuck in a cramped seat on a flight that won't leave the runway, in total misery. She shuts her eyes tight and tries to visualize a better airplane situation: a spacious seat, a soft pillow, a kind and lovely steward…but BOOM…she's woken by a nudging. Jane reluctantly

opens her eyes but is surprised by the lovely face of a flight attendant (wearing the uniform of the airline you're trying to sell). The flight attendant smiles and gently nudges Jane again with the soft pillow she requested. Jane accepts it only to notice that she is (as she dreamed) now in a much more spacious and comfortable seat. The flight attendant smiles again and says, "Time for takeoff." Jane snuggles into her pillow on her spacious seat and closes her eyes again, this time with a peaceful smile as the plane departs.

I'm the first to admit, it's not exactly Shakespeare, but your brain wants to make connections between characters, and it loves to resolve conflict in stories. Begin with those meaningful ideas or images that you've circled and start to daydream. *No, you can't daydream while scrolling through Instagram.* Close your eyes, talk to yourself, pace the room, stand under the shower, make yourself a bit bored, but keep focused on the four or five ideas that you've circled in your notes. The story is already up there; you just need to allow your mind time to put together a narrative in a way that works for you.

## On writing

Don't worry, I'm not going to get into a whole thing about writing. There are a million books written by prizewinners on the subject. The only advice I'm going to give comes from Ernest Hemingway, who knows a thing or two about stringing words together. He says, "The first draft of anything is [BLEEP]!" If that's true, then why worry? As you get into the following writing assignments don't stress out, just get those words down on paper; there's plenty of time to edit, so don't worry if it all sounds like BLEEP!

## Hone Your Pitch

**Don't go in the water.** —Tagline for the film *Jaws* (1975)

Five words. That's all it took to boil down Steven Spielberg's blockbuster film about a man-eating great white shark that terrorizes beachgoers at a small summer resort. But believe it or not, to get those five words, the tagline's author needed to know exactly what the project was about and whom it was for.

*At this point, so do you.*

Mind you, you're not creating a tagline to promote some million-dollar product or some multi-billion–dollar film. Instead, you'll use your tagline as a means to better understand your own work. Writing a tagline forces you to know your project *intimately* and, just as important, kicks off a commitment to a branding process for your project.

Before you can come up with a tagline, however, you'll need to craft your *elevator pitch*. Here, you're getting ready for the muse's second visit; you want her to be perfectly satisfied with your planning and preparation. First, write down what you want the *tone* of your piece to be. That is, how would you want people to describe it? Should they be saying that it's heartfelt, scary, funny, dramatic, informative? Is it quirky, melancholic, outrageous, urban, loud? Throw the best tonal words up on the wall.

Next, write down the *plot* of your story in a sentence or two. Plot is what the story is "about." For *Jaws*, "a great white shark terrorizes a small beach town until a brave group of shark hunters go on the offensive." Make it simple and, really, two sentences max.

Underneath the plot, you'll work with theme. *Theme* is the deep message of your story that you may not even plan. Write down various themes of the story, that is, what your story is "really about." For *Jaws*, this could be "man versus nature," "fear of the unknown," or "human vulnerability." What's cool about theme is that it can be interpreted in many ways, so you can make whatever interpretation suits you as long as it makes sense to your story. A simple love story may end up being really about cowardice or about gratitude. It's up to you to identify what your piece is "really about" deep down; you're going to need to figure that out and put it on the wall.

Finally, write one sentence combining the three concepts to become the elevator pitch: "*Jaws* is a *terrifying* movie (tone) that *pits a man-eating shark against a small beach town* (plot) with an underlying *man versus nature* idea (theme)." Okay, you have now organized your story into tone, plot, and theme. Beautiful! You're fully organized and ready to move on to your tagline.

If you're very lucky, the words will already be in your elevator pitch. For instance, regarding the first love story we discussed previously, you may focus on the untied shoelaces and go with a simple tagline like "Love, Untied" or maybe something about the boy being messy like "First Love Can Be Messy."

The good things about a tagline is that you can use it as a guide as you're creating your project, and if you use the tagline for promotion, the viewer's expectations will pretty much match the story: The tone is going to be sweet, it's going to be about love, and you get the sense that things won't go perfectly (but won't go horribly wrong, either).

For the airline ad (and I must remind you that we're not looking for a tagline for the *airline*, just your piece), you may focus on the word "takeoff" and Jane's daydream of a better seat. Maybe "Takeoff as You Imagined" or, even focusing on the spaciousness of the seat, "Dream Bigger." There is some wordplay that goes into it; Google does help in this instance, but try not to get caught up in being too witty. Again, clarity is the key—or as branding folks love to say (but often fail to achieve): "Clarity over cleverness." When the muse shows, you're done with preparations; concept development is complete.

## PREVISUALIZATION
### *What does it look like?*

Look at you! You've nailed your story to a few simple words, and that's essential for you to move on to the next step of pre-production.

*Previsualization* is also referred to as visual development or concept art. And FYI, folks in the business call it *previs* for short. Whatever you call it, this stage helps define the *look and feel* of your production before it begins. Previsualization can range from simple sketches to fully rendered characters and backgrounds. Previs serves to both solidify design direction as well as establish animation techniques and methods. It gives you the opportunity to experiment with visual directions, materials, and animation. We've discussed tone, plot, and theme, but how do you want your project to *look* and *feel*? Will people describe it as graphic, textural, clean, gritty, minimal, edgy, vintage? Will your project have a handmade aesthetic or will it be more simple and mechanical? Getting the look and feel right is the first step in expressing your idea visually.

**Cody Walzel,** Sketchbook Art

## Be influenced

I'd love to tell you just to close your eyes and dream up a look and feel that's uniquely yours. If you can, by all means do so. You may already have a firm grasp on how you want your piece to look and feel. But it's okay to be influenced, and there should be no shame in checking out how other artists have done things in the past. I mean, you probably got into animation because you loved someone else's work, so why shut yourself off to that influence now? When I tell you to jump on the Internet and watch lots of motion graphics and animated shorts and commercials, have fun, but remember that you are doing real work here. This is research, so I don't want to catch you binge watching Old Spice commercials on YouTube and forgetting the plan (though that Terry Crews guy is hilarious!). The biggest mistake artists make is not spending time looking for good references; in other words, don't set out to make something totally original without looking for influences. In order to make something truly fresh, you must study what has been done before, and that means finding those references.

Create a file on your computer called "References" and in it collect screenshots of the images you find online that you like or feel are pertinent to your piece.

Maybe one piece has a color treatment that appeals to you or a visual rhythm or story structure that feels right. Fill the file with lots of things you want to be influenced by. Think about what exactly draws you to each piece and let that guide the direction of your project. If you want, write down those thoughts.

## Experiment

*Oh, muse? We need you again! You're busy? Shucks...*

Oh well, we've got to do this one on our own. But guess what? We'll do just fine without her because we're learning to be more organized. Warning: It might get a little messy!

First, step away from the computer again! I firmly believe that the best experimentation happens in the physical world. After all that time Googling and grabbing images online, your mind will respond to the tactile. And you should get a little bit DIY here. Grab some colored pencils, cardboard, watercolors, cotton balls, sandpaper, Play-Doh, crayons, coffee grinds... basically raid a kindergarten class and throw on a messy sweatshirt. Oh, and music, because as we all know, music helps spike creativity. So blast it—and if your neighbors threaten to call the cops, settle for headphones.

# EXPERI MENTING — WITH — DESIGN

Now get wild: Draw with your left hand, spill coffee, melt crayons, let yourself be inventive. Think about some of the images in your piece and deconstruct them in an effort to see things from another angle. You may be surprised how freeing it is to treat design like a science experiment.

## Impact your story with design

I know I told you way back in the beginning of this chapter that your story was getting sealed up, but that's not to say it can't evolve. Doing the kind of previsualization work that you've done so far will inevitably impact your story. Animators and motion artists often go back and forth between designing and refining their concept and the story beats (more on this in the next chapter). This happens because previsualization forces you to point a magnifying glass on the primary images of your story. A dragon that you created for your antacid commercial to represent tummy troubles might work better with a goofy-face design: Suddenly you realize that the dragon doesn't have to be the nasty fire-breathing kind and instead can be nutty and clumsy. Your brave knight may decide to play a trick on the silly dragon instead of violently lancing him with a sword. That's an example of story changing due to visual development. Be prepared and flexible for the design process to inform this concept development. It's an essential part of the storytelling process.

If your story does change as a result of visual concept development, please go back and change your elevator pitch and (if you need to) even your tagline to match. Sorry!

Sincerely, The Management.

# ASSET BUILDING
## *What is it made of?*

*Assets* are all of the pieces you'll need to begin animating. Assets could range from logos, character designs, replacement pieces, props, backgrounds, live action files, fonts, color scripts, sound effects, and more. All of the "stuff" you'll need to go in there and make the magic happen. While you won't be able to finalize your assets before creating your storyboard and script (which we'll tackle in the next chapters), you can get started on asset building and creating an organization system with well-marked files. And, who knows? You might be lucky and already have some assets that you made here in previsualization that you'll end up using in your final piece.

Guess what? You've completed the important steps of pre-production! Pretty soon you'll be off and running, animating through the night, headed for fame, fortune, and a shelf full of awards. And I'm sure you've internalized *everything* we've gone over, right? As a reminder, here are the important steps of pre-production.

## PRE-PRODUCTION RECAP

1. Write a creative brief.
2. Identify your big idea and create a storyline.
3. Develop an elevator pitch and tagline.
4. Determine your project's look and feel through influence and experimenting with design directions.
5. Make changes to your story based on design decisions.
6. Begin building and organizing your assets.

**Sirirat Yoom Thawilvejakul**, *Music Studio*

## ASSIGNMENT
Create an advertisement for a place

Now let's try a short assignment where you get to create your own advertisement.

Using all of the steps we've learned in this chapter, take a stab at pre-production on an advertisement for TV. Create a 20-second ad for a place (real or imagined): a city, state, country, mall, zoo, bar, bowling alley, planet, or the like. The goal is to make it feel like somewhere people would actually want to go. The demographic you're reaching and the reason for them wanting to go there are completely up to you.

You can flesh out your concept using the eight frames below to communicate your concept with a beginning, middle, and end.

# 2

# STORYTELLING

## Tame the limitless medium

There are lots of reasons to love telling stories using animation. But the best reason? There are no limits. You can break the rules of gravity, toss aside the space-time continuum, invent impossible worlds, and take your audience on a journey simply with shapes, sounds, and colors. Want a glorious swirling moment in human history to take place on a single blade of grass? Go for it. Want people to *literally* wear their hearts on their sleeves? It's your world! Anything is possible and anything goes.

With such possibility comes the opportunity to stretch the limits of your imagination and indulge in the medium's boundless world. *But do you think your mind hasn't the capacity to create never-before-seen worlds?* Think about the last dream you had—likely it broke all sorts of laws of physics, and maybe even morality! Your mind is a deep well of the impossible and is boundlessly creative, I assure you.

First we'll cover a standard storytelling model, followed later by "non-narrative storytelling" in which I'll encourage you to see for yourself how far beyond the bounds you can go: You'll be prompted to tell two stories, one straightforward and the other like a jazz riff, a post-modern poem, a dreamscape that takes audiences on an unpredictable and even uncomfortable voyage. I will encourage you to go hog wild.

But the great challenge in creating meaningful animated stories is less about letting your imagination fly free. We know it can do that. *The great challenge is more about disciplining yourself to reel it in and be intentional about your storytelling choices.* Because what is most consistent among well-crafted animated stories is less how mind-bending of a world the artist created but more how much discipline they exercised in limiting their choices, especially as it pertains to storytelling. With this chapter we'll follow two storytelling paths that allow for disciplined creativity.

# STORY STRUCTURE

In the last chapter you summoned the storytelling muse and established your narrative idea. You even whittled down your story idea into a few choice words. Now it's time to plot that baby out and see where the story "beats" are.

## You've Got the Beats

*Beats* are all the moments or active steps that move your story forward, and "plotting them out" means laying down those beats into an order that creates the most emotional impact. Every writer's room in America uses good old-fashioned cue cards to plot out story and record the beats. Cue cards have a magical quality because they can be moved around, thrown out, and amended in seconds. They remind us that stories are malleable and that no card is precious until they're all in their final order. So please step away from your sparkling 27-inch retina monitor, grab a pack of three-dollar cue cards, and let's get to work.

***Artist's Note:*** *If sketching out your beats on the cue cards is more intuitive for you than writing, then by all means sketch your beats. Just make sure that the sketches are rough enough that you don't mind throwing them out later.*

On your stack of cue cards, go ahead and write down/sketch out all of the moments that move your story along until the conclusion. Each card should represent an active step or beat in the storyline and can be both physical and/or emotional. For example, suppose you have a story of a lion hunting for food. *The lion stalking prey* is an active step, as is *the lion feels hungry.* Treat each of these beats as the same level of importance for now. And don't worry too much if you haven't figured out the specifics of how you will show these beats yet. Your cards might read "Lion stalks prey" and "Show that lion is hungry." You jot these down on the card, even though you may not yet have figured out how to show the hunt and if you want your lion's tummy to rumble or you want to express his hunger in another way. For a short animated piece, you should end up with a nice little stack, between 15 and 30 cards in total.

## Three-Act Structure: Problems Solved

Now that you've got your stack of cue cards that encompass every element of what happens in your story, place those on the wall in chronological order in three separate rows. These three rows represent a traditional *three-act storytelling structure,* which, at its most distilled, is a linear story with three basic steps or acts (and is perfectly suited to shorts): 1. A character has a problem. 2. The character works towards a solution. 3. The character solves the problem, usually in a surprising way (see the Three-Act Story Structure chart that follows). Next, create a fourth row of "additional beats." You'll put cards here that either don't fit into your structure or that you simply don't yet know what to do with (and which you may never use). Note on theme: We'll talk more about theme later, but do keep your story's theme in mind as you create these cue cards. Whether you incorporate that theme as you go along or you go back and supplement the cards later, theme will play an important part in the storytelling process.

These three steps form the fundamental arc of a traditional short story. Three-act structure is so engrained in us as human beings that it permeates even the most common storytelling medium: jokes. Unless your beloved uncle is telling it, you probably like your jokes to get right to the point and pay off quickly. *Knock-Knock. Who's there? Nobel? Nobel who? No bell, that's why I knocked.* I sincerely apologize for exposing you to that corny joke, but it nicely illustrates the three-act structure. Here, a character has someone knocking on their door and they don't know who it is (Problem, Act 1). They ask who it is twice (Attempt to Solve Problem, Act 2). Finally, they learn who is knocking: a horrible punster (Resolution, Act 3).

**NOTE FOR MOTION GRAPHICS ARTISTS**
Three-act structure works for information-oriented motion graphics, too. While you may not be working with "characters" that are aiming to "solve problems," you will likely have a "question" that "needs to be answered." For example in a PSA, a question might be: "Breast Cancer is taking more and more lives. How do we raise money for research?" Use the Three-Act Story Structure graph to map out three-act structure for both animation and motion graphics.

## Act 1: Setting up character and conflict

Your first row of cue cards, Act 1, should introduce your character(s), establish what they want, and also introduce a problem standing in the way of them getting what they want. Some examples are: A stork is very late to deliver his daily quota of babies, but he's so easily distractible that he's never going to make the deadline. A tree wants sunlight, but it's locked in a dark closet. A boy wants to eat a delicious bowl of soup, but he doesn't have a spoon. By the end of Act 1 you should have established your character's problem and what stands in the way of them solving it. There should be the sense that solving the problem is going to take some serious effort.

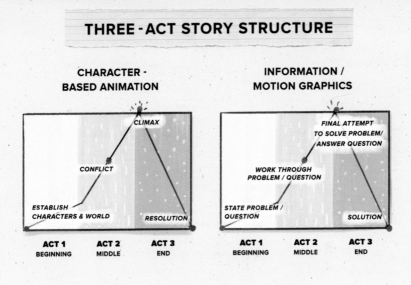

# THREE-ACT STORY STRUCTURE

**CHARACTER-BASED ANIMATION**

CLIMAX

CONFLICT

ESTABLISH CHARACTERS & WORLD

RESOLUTION

| ACT 1 | ACT 2 | ACT 3 |
|-------|-------|-------|
| BEGINNING | MIDDLE | END |

**INFORMATION / MOTION GRAPHICS**

FINAL ATTEMPT TO SOLVE PROBLEM/ ANSWER QUESTION

WORK THROUGH PROBLEM / QUESTION

STATE PROBLEM / QUESTION

SOLUTION

| ACT 1 | ACT 2 | ACT 3 |
|-------|-------|-------|
| BEGINNING | MIDDLE | END |

## Act 2: Working towards a solution

The next row of cards, Act 2, is where the character attempts to overcome the problem. Here your character fully commits to solving their problem and comes up against all sorts of roadblocks that make solving it seem even less likely.

I cannot tell you how much easier this step will be if you take the time to flesh out your main character with specifics. In our story of the distractible stork, what else can we know about him? What if he is vain about his moustache… and he is always hoping to find his long-lost sister? How about if our stork loves Latin jazz? Suddenly, your story has many possibilities for Act 2. We know from Act 1 that our stork has only a limited amount of time to deliver his babies and so is trying hard to ward off his proclivity towards distraction. But what will distract our stork? What will be the roadblocks preventing him from accomplishing his goal? Well, now that we know him a bit better, wouldn't it seem fitting if he's continually distracted by waxing his moustache in mirrored buildings? Maybe he keeps thinking he sees his long-lost sister in passing apartments, or perhaps he even closes his eyes to enjoy some Tito Puente and loses track of time? The more specific traits you give your character, the more opportunities you will have to create organic roadblocks for them in

Act 2. So please ask some specific questions of your main character: What are their distinguishing physical attributes? What do they love? Hate? What is their driving motivation in life? Their secret? Their biggest fear, and so on?

## Act 3: Attaining the big solve

Okay, so our distractible stork has committed to solving his problem (delivering those babies on time) and is working hard towards that goal, but he keeps coming up against roadblocks that make attaining his goal nearly impossible. By the last card in Act 2 you should have the feeling that there's a good chance the problem will NOT be solved (your character has tried almost everything). But there is still that one in a million chance…

Your third row of cards, Act 3, is the resolution. This act usually has fewer cards than Acts 1 and 2 because the character should now be facing their problem head on, winding into an unexpected resolution. In our story about the distracted stork, the deadline is almost up. He has one baby left but has accidentally locked himself into an apartment where he thought he saw his long-lost sister. He's doomed! *So what's going to happen?* What will be the satisfying ending to your story? Will he magically stumble upon the parents of the last baby and deliver it in time? Will he fail to meet the deadline and be fired from his job? Will a certain jazz song on the radio (his long-lost sister's favorite) remind him of the importance of uniting family, thereby infusing him with a sudden ability to hyper-focus? Will he pry open the apartment window and fly directly to the baby's home just in time to make the delivery before midnight *and* discover his long-lost sister playing jazz trumpet in the backyard?

The choice of best ending rests squarely on you establishing exactly what it is you're *trying to say* with your story. Creating a satisfying ending requires more information than just the beats you've written down under Acts 1, 2, and 3. On the board is what your story is "about," which is the overall plot, the beats, the scenes. But in order to create a truly satisfying ending you also need to know what your story is "really about," or *the theme*. We talked about this a bit in the first chapter, but I can't stress enough how important it is for you to establish what *deep down* message you're trying to explore with your story.

In our stork-y… sorry… story about the stork, how we end the story depends on the message we want to give or point we want to make. For instance, if our

theme is optimistic, like "love conquers all," then, indeed, it's the moment when our stork is focused on his love for his sister that he finally finds the strength to do his job. This uplifting theme drives towards a happy ending, so you expect him to be reunited. If, however, you decide that your story has a dark perspective on life, like "love causes pain," then our stork would fail to reach his baby-delivering deadline, be fired from his job, end up alone listening to his jazz, and forever longing for his sister. Not great for the babies but still a satisfying ending that is enriched by theme.

But don't stop at a great ending. As I've said above, theme should enrich your entire narrative. Go back to your cards and jot down some notes on how your message can enhance each beat in your story. If you have an optimistic theme, "love conquers all," the neighborhood might be sunlit and colorful, surrounded by lush parks where cats purr lovingly as the stork makes his deliveries to snappy jazz. If you have a dark story and your theme is "love causes pain," the neighborhoods where the stork delivers might be mysterious with angry dogs in the windows; the lighting would be dramatic, with muted colors; and your piece might have sad jazz music.

### Three-act structure, example one

Phil Borst's one-minute short film *Color Blind* (see images from the film below) is a great example of simple Three-Act Story structure infused with theme. When asked what his story is about, Mr. Borst said, "The underlying theme of the story is *kindness* and how sometimes a person in need can easily be overlooked because they are a little different."

Act 1. Blue Square, who lives in a world of happy, rolling circles, is unhappy because he's a square and cannot roll. Act 2. Pink Circle stops next to the

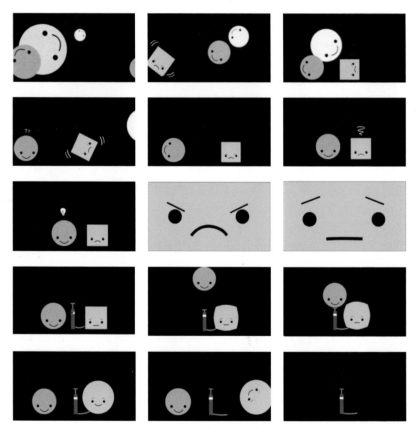

**Phil Borst**, *Color Blind*

Blue Square and for a moment appears to have a helpful idea. This gives Blue Square hope. But just as quickly Pink Circle rolls off, leaving Blue Square alone again and even more unhappy! Act 3. But Pink Circle returns…with a bicycle pump! She pumps Blue Square with air until he becomes a circle that can roll. Blue Square is delighted and thankful for Pink Circle's kindness. They both roll away, happy.

The plot is easy to pin down, but notice how Borst's theme, *kindness,* permeates throughout the piece. Take Pink Circle's size, for instance. She's not the smallest of the circles; if she was, we might think that she's just a child motivated more by naiveté than kindness. She's also not the biggest of circles, which might insinuate that she's acting on a kind of Alpha generosity. Also notice that once Pink Circle blows up Blue Square, Blue Square is actually a bit bigger than Pink Circle, not the same size or smaller. If Blue Square ended up being the exactly same size, you might think that Pink Square was motivated to create a perfect playmate for herself—that would be about friendship and not just kindness. That idea is reinforced by the fact that Pink Circle and Blue Square don't roll off in the same direction. They go off happily in separate directions. Borst wanted to give the impression of selfless kindness, with no strings attached or expectations. Pink Circle simply sees Blue Square struggling and wants to be kind.

### Three-act structure, example two

*Heart* is a United Airlines commercial directed by the brilliant animation director Jamie Caliri (see images from the film on the next pages). A master of visual storytelling, Caliri's stories always feel more inevitable than predictable. The audience is along for the ride, always rooting for the character to reach their goal.

Act 1. Two lovers say goodbye at the airport and the woman gives the man her heart to keep while she's gone. Her problem is that she needs to get back to this man who has her heart (literally and figuratively). Act 2. The woman flies off to accomplish the work she needs to get done before she can return to the man. It's hard work and she feels empty; after all, her heart is missing. Act 3. The woman returns to the man who gently hands her back her heart. She is whole again and they can be together.

**Jamie Caliri**, United Airlines, *Heart*

There are many themes that can be attributed to this piece, but let's take a swing at the bat: "When you love someone you aren't whole without them." Or maybe the inverse: "Togetherness makes you whole." It's a sweet message but doesn't have to be interpreted as happy-go-lucky. You can see by the way the female character gazes longingly out the airplane window that Caliri sees some sadness in the notion that people are not quite whole without being next to the one they love. Notice that in the end the female character does not run headlong into the arms of her lover, elated to have her heart back. She is simply happy to see him again—more comforted than ecstatic.

# NONLINEAR
# STORY STRUCTURE

Okay, like I promised earlier in this chapter, it's time to go a bit hog wild. Because while traditional three-act structure provides a dependable method for creating animated stories, what if you want something that offers just a little bit more…? Sound *dangerous?*

What if you're influenced by stories that don't seem to have recognizable arcs or easily interpreted thematic intentions? What if you want to tell stories that cut between different points in time, are whimsical, moody, and symbolic, and use sound, color, and pacing in a totally unexpected way?

Still interested? Then *nonlinear storytelling* may be for you. It's a treasure trove for seekers of a more poetic, non-narrative, abstract style of storytelling. And it's a blast to make. But don't be fooled. Though nonlinear storytelling may appear chaotic, it actually requires even more planning and attention to detail than linear storytelling. In nonlinear you no longer have three-act structure to guide you, and gone are the limits on how you can use character, sound, and design. You're completely without a net. Totally scary, and yet totally invigorating.

*So, how do you go about making a nonlinear story?*

## Begin with Inspiration

First, you must identify a point of departure (such as a sound, an image, or an idea) that you find so powerful that you're inspired to build around it. It must be something that makes so much sense to you, provides you with such a spark, that even the wildest interpretation of it would prove compelling to you. Whether it's a song that repeats in your head, a poem you once heard that blew your mind, an image from a dream you've stowed away since childhood, whatever your inspiration is, think of it as a piece of art so valuable that you must build a museum around it and open doors to the public.

But that better be some gorgeous museum, right? Because unless it meets the standard of your inspiration, then the whole thing gets sullied. And therein lies the challenge. While your inspiration may be a beautiful thing, it's not enough on its own, so it's up to you to create elements that work to elevate it. If your inspiration is a song, then the images must be just as splendid; if you need words to match, they'd better be pure poetry. Do not let your inspirational element do the heavy lifting in your piece. Let it lead by inspiring the other elements to rise up and match it.

## Now Build a Structure

Wait, wait, I thought this was time to go wild—no structure, no rules, remember?

I go wild, and I want you to go wild, too, but now that you've found your priceless piece of art and created all of the elements to build your museum, let's at least make sure that there's a roof! In the Nonlinear Story Structures chart are quick descriptions of four easy-to-follow nonlinear story structures that provide a tremendous amount of freedom…but still provide a roof for your story.

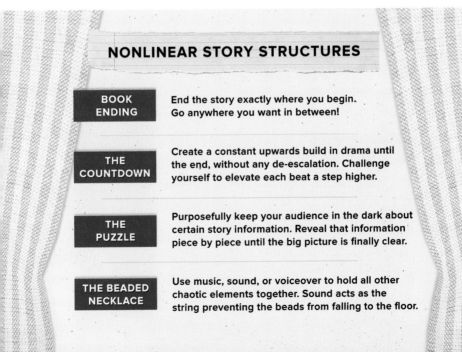

### NONLINEAR STORY STRUCTURES

| | |
|---|---|
| **BOOK ENDING** | End the story exactly where you begin. Go anywhere you want in between! |
| **THE COUNTDOWN** | Create a constant upwards build in drama until the end, without any de-escalation. Challenge yourself to elevate each beat a step higher. |
| **THE PUZZLE** | Purposefully keep your audience in the dark about certain story information. Reveal that information piece by piece until the big picture is finally clear. |
| **THE BEADED NECKLACE** | Use music, sound, or voiceover to hold all other chaotic elements together. Sound acts as the string preventing the beads from falling to the floor. |

As you can see, it's not an exact science, and yet nonlinear consists of the most prevalent animated storytelling out there: Music videos, title sequences, broadcast graphics, and title sequences for TV and film all follow nonlinear storytelling structures. While it's often considered the most "out there" and "artistic," nonlinear also consists of some of the most commercial. *That is to say, it's important you become as proficient a nonlinear storyteller as a linear one.* We all need a paycheck, after all…

## Nonlinear structure sample: The Beaded Necklace

Let's take the case study of Louis Morton's award-winning film *Passer Passer* as an example of nonlinear storytelling done just right. The film completely blew me away when I first encountered it, not that I could describe exactly what it was about. But what I could describe, quite effortlessly, was the soundtrack. It's an urban soundscape of honking and shuffling and churning metal and concrete—a cacophony of people and rhythms with great emotional power.

Notice when Morton describes his film how key his *inspiration element* was to its creation: "*Passer* is inspired by the city symphony documentary films of the 1920s. My goal was to capture the atmosphere of a city by recording its sounds and creating an imagined world inspired by those sounds. It's a playful look at the relationship between people and their built environment."

And while the structure in his film does seem chaotic, listen to how intentional Morton sounds when he describes the structural aspects of the film: "I wanted the viewer to pass through one sound environment to the next until all the sounds return at the end. In many ways the film was based more on the structure of a song than on a traditional narrative film structure."

I encourage you to track down this film online or in the festivals. It simply must be experienced and exists as a great example of nonlinear storytelling born of inspiration and infused with nonlinear structure. Take a peek at some of the images in the film shown here, which as you can see Morton elevated to meet his aural inspiration.

**Louis Morton**, *Passer Passer*

# Nonlinear structure sample: Book Ending

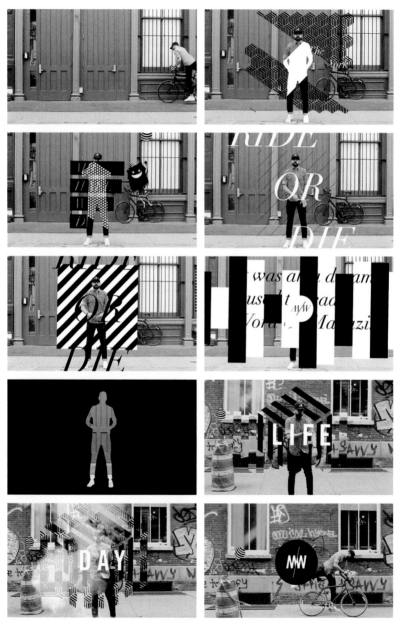

**Michael Waldron,** *Exquisite Corpse*

As you can see in some of Michael Waldron's *Exquisite Corpse* images, this is a great example of using the book ending structure to help organize a nonlinear story. His piece begins with a man riding in on a bike and ends with the same man riding off on a bike. A series of text, graphics, and even a new animated character appears in the middle, but the structure works because the story is bound together by a common book ending. The structure of similar arrival (at the top) and departure (at the end) implies that a journey has taken place in between. No matter how chaotic that journey may appear, it just make sense.

## STORYTELLING RECAP

| Three-Act Structure | Nonlinear Structure |
|---|---|
| Create the beats | Identify your inspiration |
| Build the story's arc | Create the beats |
| Act 1: Problem | Build your own structure |
| Act 2: Attempt to solve it | Use a known structure |
| Act 3: Resolution | Book Ending |
| | The Countdown |
| | The Puzzle |
| | The Beaded Necklace |

## ASSIGNMENT
Linear and nonlinear storytelling

Grab your sketchbook and, using the steps we've learned in this chapter, tell two stories about a favorite mode of transportation, one using linear three-act storytelling and another using nonlinear (that opportunity I told you you'd have for using an inspirational point of departure to go hog wild).

# STORY STARTERS

## Keep a Prolific Story Journal

When it comes to creating animated stories, quantity is key. With a little practice, you'll no longer be worried if your "perfect idea" isn't working because you'll have five more ready to go.

The first step is to get yourself a blank journal. Carry it with you and write in it compulsively. Fill it with meandering thoughts, personal experiences, snippets you eavesdrop waiting for the train, and narrative threads. Jot down embarrassing questions, odd themes, fantasies, nonsense, and so on. Don't worry if your notes are silly, crazy, or even cliché. Once a week, go through your journal and circle what catches your eye. Look for repetitive and provocative ideas that keep coming up and connections that spark new thoughts. Animated stories often come from mashing two concepts that don't seem to fit together, so pair that question you wrote about caveman chefs with your haiku on Jell-O—there just may be story gold there!

Once you've honed in on something that interests you, close your eyes and think. Your mind loves to create narratives—to solve narrative puzzles—so if you commit to focusing on only your cave dwelling chef and Jell-O rhyme for long enough, I assure you that a story kernel will appear, no matter how *disturbing* that story kernel may be. Now type that morphing idea into a document titled *Story Ideas,* and move on to the next. After a few weeks, you'll be surprised at the number of story kernels you have on your list. So many that you probably won't care if a couple don't work out.

## Story Idea...Meet Classic Plot

Ideally your list of story ideas are so groundbreaking that no stale, old structure could possibly contain them. Believe me, nothing would make me happier than if you discovered some new, brilliant way to tell stories! But in the meantime, experimenting with classic storytelling paradigms (the ones that human beings have been using since the dawn of time) never hurt anyone. You might even find it liberating.

## YOUR TURN - TRY ONE

As a test, take one of your new story kernels and pop it into one of the classic plots listed below. These plots have evolved over centuries to create immediate conflict and high stakes. Odds are pitted against protagonists in a way that may seem impossible to overcome...until, in the end, they are not.

# TIMELESS PLOTS
# WITH UNIVERSAL CONFLICTS

**GOOD VERSUS EVIL / OVERCOMING THE "MONSTER"**
Character battles against a dark force to save himself or his community. *(Star Wars)*

**REBIRTH AND REDEMPTION** Villain spirals towards darkness, finds need to change before it's too late. *(Beauty and the Beast)*

**RAGS TO RICHES** Trapped in a world of poverty, hero uses cunning, good character, and some luck to acquire great wealth and power. *(Charlie and the Chocolate Factory)*

**ROLE REVERSALS** Character steps into shoes of another, gains new perspective, which affects those around him. *(Aladdin)*

**BUDDY STORIES** Two (or more) characters with opposing personalities work to solve a problem. *(Toy Story)*

**LOVE STORIES** Two lovers come together against the will of a powerful force trying to pull them apart. *(Sleeping Beauty)*

**QUEST / JOURNEYS / VOYAGE AND RETURN** Hero sets out on journey to find something he really wants. When he finds it, it's not what he expected but learns a rich lesson. *(Wizard of Oz)*

**SHIP OF FOOLS** A group of misfits goes on a comedic adventure and learns lessons along the way. *(Ice Age)*

**THE REBEL / LIFE AGAINST THE GRAIN** Rebel, who is castigated for being different, saves community using the very trait that distinguishes him. *(Happy Feet)*

**COMING OF AGE** A character transitions from childhood to adulthood and learns lessons along the way. *(Lion King)*

# 3

# STORYBOARDING
## Build your visual script

*"At our studio we don't write our stories, we draw them."*
—*Walt Disney*

Walt Disney is known for many important innovations in the field of animation and motion graphics. But perhaps his most useful contribution came in the 1930s when he decided to pin up a series of his rough sketches in sequence to help explain a story idea to his team. Like many great innovations, the decision came out of necessity—animation is an expensive and time-consuming process in which a single misstep can be very costly. Being able to solidify story before animating could potentially save a fledgling animation studio like Disney's more than a few bucks. Plus, the method suited Mr.

Disney's natural showmanship. He used the visual aid of his sketches to bring the full scope of his ideas to life, including his thoughts on timing, staging, framing, continuity, and transitions. He would use these sketches to get people excited—from his team of artists to potential investors. The process became essential at Disney, and within ten years live-action studios caught on as well, making storyboarding as ubiquitous as scripts in Hollywood backlots.

Storyboarding is your opportunity to work out the visual elements that best suit your story. It can help you determine most aspects of your animated piece before moving a single pixel. Boarding saves time and money and can help you get people excited about your project before it's made. Simply put, the better your storyboard, the more likely you are to achieve success with your project.

**PLEASE NOTE**

This chapter presents the classic, commercial storyboarding process. Many animators use the storyboarding process to "write" their story—this chapter assumes you've arrived here with a fleshed-out story. Many motion graphics artists prefer to tackle timing early on in their process and therefore might jump from thumbnail sketches straight to digital animatic. While this chapter lays out a specific process, I encourage you to personalize your own and find what works best for you!

I'll cover the basic structure of storyboarding first and then continue on with some of the details you'll use throughout the process that allow you to make your storyboard complete and ready for animatics. The entire process is organic; let your storyboarding evolve gradually from simple to more complex.

# BUILD THE STORYBOARD

As you begin the process of storyboarding, you're creating individual frames of the action. You start out rough and gradually add the needed details. This process ensures the story is first understandable and then allows you to add the nuances that make the story more complex and interesting.

## Thumbnailing

*Thumbnails* are the first rough sketches of your storyboards. They help you work out the sequencing of your "shots" and provide an opportunity to establish important aspects of staging, framing, scale, and transitions. Your thumbnail drawings should be rough—stick figures are just fine. Use Post-it Notes as well—they're re-positionable and purposefully limit the amount of detail you can add to your drawing. Approach thumbnailing as the experimentation phase of storyboarding, and keep a wastebasket nearby— you're going to be lobbing a lot of hook shots in that general direction.

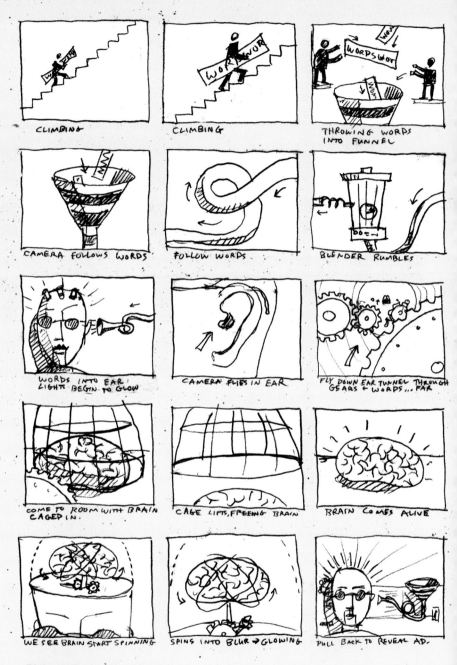

**Richard Borge**, Storyboard Art

### Thumbnail revisions

Once you've drawn up your thumbnail sketches, slap them up on the wall in sequence and get ready for some brutal revisions. Do the shots make sense? Are there leaps in time or logic? Lags in story? Clunky flow from scene to scene? Pitch your thumbnails to yourself frame-by-frame and voice out any dialogue you've written, or even sing the music you intend to play over the finished piece. If something isn't working, be ruthless. Stick a Post-it® Note over problem areas and re-draw until it feels right. Any fixes you make here will save you time and heartache down the road.

## Storyboarding

If thumbnailing was about rough stick figures, then *storyboarding* is about... *stick figures with bowties?* What!? Some storyboard artists take the time to create beautifully polished renditions of each frame, but the goal here is not high art, it's clarity. If you are able to capture the action and emotion of your story with little more than scribbles, then go for it, but just make sure you're able to capture all the detail. Just don't come crying to me when you start animating and say, "Wait, I forgot his hat! My chef has no hat, but there's no room to add it!"

Once you've completed your drawings, use the space underneath each frame to write either dialogue or brief explanatory notes (such as, "hears bear" or "comes to life"). Once you're done, a casual observer should be able to understand what's going on in each frame and even follow the overall story.

### Storyboard revisions

Time to test out your storyboards by presenting them to a small audience or, at very least, in front of one person who isn't afraid to ask you hard questions. Pitching your storyboard to an audience will force you to clarify your beats and the decisions you've made about staging and flow. Plus, an authentic human reaction offers a great sounding board. Watch your audiences' body language as you pitch—it's as important as (and often more honest than) their verbal feedback.

Once you've made changes based on feedback, revise your boards and clean them up for public consumption. Many clients will react better to clean, elegantly rendered storyboards. If a client needs to be sold on an idea from boards alone, they better sparkle! If a crew of animators and designers are using your boards to generate their shot list, then the boards should be detailed enough so that no element is left up to interpretation.

**NOTE ON STYLE**

Consider using a distinct drawing style to enhance your storyboards. If your piece is humorous, consider a lighter, cartoony style. If your project is full of drama, black and white coloring might work best. If it's especially sophisticated, layering in baroque detail may help to enhance your vision. Choose well—style choices that you make in the storyboarding phase can help clarify your intentions and bring your story to life.

## STORYBOARDING HINTS

Okay, now that you know the steps to set up the basic structure of your storyboards, what's the best method for creating effective storyboards? Or in other words, what are the details you need to consider throughout the storyboard process to allow you to add the visual elements that will bring the full scope of *your* story to life? It has a lot to do with putting on your director's hat. You have to compose your "shots" as in a movie, not only for clarity (which is the most important thing) but also for maximum emotional impact. That means learning a thing of two about shot composition, framing, staging, and transitions. These are the details that you add frame by frame making each a perfect unit as they allow the complete story to unfold.

**Sterling Sheehy**, Storyboards

## Shot Composition

Want to give your audience the feel of a majestic location—say, a mountain peak at sunset? A slow, *panning extreme wide shot* will evoke the mountain's beauty and sheer size. What about the lone climber who finally reaches the summit of that mountain? How best to capture their joy? A *close-up* will best reveal the expression on their face (and tears in their eyes) with maximum intimacy. Your audience is hungry for information, and shot composition is all about revealing information to your audience. You can get as close to, or as far away from, a subject as you want (as director you have the power of X-ray vision, flight, and invisibility all at once), so take the initiative to bring your audience right up to the action.

But composing different sized shots isn't only about providing information for your audience. It can also be used to *withhold information* for maximum effect. Take our mountain climber who has reached the peak. Let's say we choose a *medium close-up* to give the impression that she has finally reached the peak. We show our climber weeping in triumph, jumping up and down in victory—she has defeated the great mountain. But then we pull back to a *wide shot* to reveal that in fact our climber has only hiked a tiny foothill at the base of the great mountain and is nowhere near the summit! With one quick change in shot size, our climber went from skilled and heroic climbing veteran to hopeless amateur. One size change to comedy gold.

Shot composition grants you the power to reveal information how you wish to your audience, so use your power with great care.

## Framing

If sizing your shots is all about giving your audience the pertinent visual information they need, then *framing* is all about keeping that eye interested. Framing is the artistry of your shots, the "cinematography," and, in a way, the poetry. Sure, you could just plop your subject in the middle of each frame, hell, you could plop a tornado in the middle of your storyboard frame and, yes, it will still be a tornado. But you want people to feel the wind, the chaos, and the movement of the tornado. Dynamic framing is one of the keys to enhancing the visual drama in your story.

The famed "rule of thirds" provides an easy-to-follow tool for keeping your framing dynamic. Simply break down your single frame into nine equally sized quadrants by dividing it both horizontally and vertically into thirds. Now, instead of placing your subject squat in the middle (which is considered a "static" location), place it in another box—the top, bottom, left, or right third of the frame. Try laying the focal point of your subject on one of the four "intersection points" where your quadrant lines meet.

*Why do this, right? Seems random?* Well, think of it as entertaining a child on Easter Sunday. If you want them to find an Easter egg, you wouldn't just put it on the table in front of them. Since the child will naturally roam around for the Easter egg, they will likely be more excited by the egg once they find it under the park bench. It's interactive. Same with the subject in your shot. The eye wants to roam and will feel more gratified if it goes searching and finds your subject. Place your subject in the middle and there's nowhere to go—it's a boring game. Put your subject closer to the edges and there's room to roam. Play the game by the rules (of thirds) and your shots will feel more pleasurable for the eye and will give your story a sense of excitement and suspense.

# RULE OF THIRDS

**TOO CENTERED**          **MORE INTERESTING**

## Staging

While thoughtful framing helps you compose shots around a subject in a way that keeps the viewer's eye interested, *staging* is all about where you put that subject in space (and the other objects in the shot) in the scene in relation to the camera. Staging should create a visual and conceptual hierarchy for the objects and characters in your frame, placing them in a way that reinforces your overall story.

First thing to consider (as always) is clarity. You want your audience's eye to clearly see what's going on with your subject. So that means avoid crowding it with unnecessary visual information. Let's say your project is about an animator who's been up all night working on storyboards. Though their studio may have a big bookshelf or a stereo or heavily framed photos that are organic to the location, adding them to your shot means that your audience's eye will roam to story *dead zones*—where visual information does not enhance your story. You want to stage only the visual elements that will enhance your story. In the case of our animator pulling an all-nighter, you may want to stage a waste bin filled to the brim with crumpled pages next to her desk, a row of empty coffee cups on the floor, and/or an alarm clock that says 6:00 a.m. in big red letters to the side. Staging items around your subject should help to emphasize the idea you're trying to convey, while not detracting from the importance of your primary subject.

But staging has advantages beyond enhancing your subject. It can also provide *depth* to your shots. In the tangible sense, staging your subject gives a sense of physical depth to the environment. Let's look at another example for this one. One character is handing car keys to another character. Placing the characters hands and keys large in the foreground and the car small in the background will immediately create depth and interest. This staging allows the audience's eye to roam from the larger main subject to the background where it can discover the car. As mentioned earlier with the rule of thirds, discovery is a lot more pleasurable for the eye than instant gratification. Giving the eye some physical depth to explore for new information makes for a more interesting visual composition.

## SHOT INTENTION: ALL - NIGHTER ON A DEADLINE

**TOO MUCH INFO
AMBIGUOUS FOCAL POINT**

✔**BETTER**

## SHOT INTENTION: HAND - OFF KEYS TO CAR

**TOO MUCH INFO
AMBIGUOUS FOCAL POINT**

✔**BETTER**

But there is another way that staging adds depth to your shots: in the story sense. By staging your subject along with important visual information, you offer your audience a deeper read of what's happening in your story. In the case of the animator, the crumpled papers in the waste bin, of course, represent the animator's trial and error, but a deeper analysis could interpret that the overflowed waste bin represents her indomitable spirit. You must earn this leap through consistent storytelling, but once your audience gets to interpreting visual information, you may be surprised at some of the connections they make. This is generally why people call a good story "deep."

# TRANSITIONS AND CONTINUITY

*Bold statement alert:* Animation's most powerful advantage over other forms of filmmaking is the animated transition. There, I said it, caution to the wind! Anything can happen in between two frames of animation. You can transform the black pupil of an eye into the black text on a girl's report card, a fire-breathing dragon into a baby's bath toy, or the door to your boss' office into the gates of hell. As with animation as a whole, the possibilities for animated transitions are endless, which is exactly why you must practice great discipline and make those transitions work with your story. The most dependable way to ace your transitions is to pay close attention to continuity.

Continuity is the natural flow of visual information from one shot to another employed to support your story. At its most basic you must ensure that the story is flowing from shot to shot. If a character is blasted with wind in one shot, make sure that their hair is messy in the next shot and that it stays messy until they comb it. If a character is on the second floor of a building, they can't run out of the front door and into the street without walking down some stairs. You'd be surprised how many films let this stuff slip through the cracks. The simplest way to guard against continuity errors is to always follow the logic of the world you've created (spatial continuity), the story you're telling (temporal continuity), and the physical direction it's headed in (directional continuity).

## Observe Spatial Continuity

Making sure that the rules that you've established in your world are consistent from shot to shot is called *spatial continuity*. If you establish early on in your story that there is forest behind a boy's house, when he runs out of his house and into the backyard, you know where he's headed—into the woods. If you have established the size of his bedroom, when he lies on his bed throwing a ball against the wall, even if it's "off-screen," the audience should know roughly how far that ball should travel before it bounces back. Or not! Because using the wonders of animation, let's say you want to transport the boy from his bedroom directly into outer space. One great way to do that would be for the boy to throw the ball against the wall and for it never to return. Thanks to laws of spatial continuity, the audience will know that the ball should return within a second or so—when it doesn't, they can guess that either something intercepted it or (suddenly) the wall is gone! When you cut to the boy's bed surrounded by outer space, it will actually make sense as a transition since it follows the laws of spatial continuity. You'd be surprised how many professional films mess this up as well, so take the time to do a dummy check to ensure that all of your shots follow the physical world that you've created.

## Observe Temporal Continuity

The consistency of logic in your story is known as *temporal continuity*. Animation audiences will go along with dramatic visual change from shot to shot so long as it's loyal to the story they're being told. Temporal continuity can occur chronologically, or even with flashbacks or flash-forwards, but it must make sense and be earned based on the work you've done to set up a solid story. If you've established a love-struck teenager searching at a party for the object of their affections, when they finally find the person, temporal continuity will allow a variety of plausible options. You may see the teen's eyeballs transform into hearts; you may see a flashback as the teen's entire life flashes before their eyes; a flash-forward fantasy may occur that takes you years into the future as the teen stands blushing at the alter finally marrying his crush. Transitions can take wild leaps and will be easy for your audience to stomach so long as they're consistent with the story you've been telling. If your transition doesn't make sense to the audience, then you haven't earned that leap—so head back to the storyboard.

## Observe Directional Continuity

This final rule is pretty simple with *directional continuity*. Maintain the direction of any action for an object or character in a sequence from shot to shot. If a car is driving from the left side of a panel to the right, you must continue that same movement into your next shot. Switching directions of vehicles, characters, or any object that is headed in a particular direction is disorienting to the viewer and a big no-no in storyboarding. Do a second dummy check here, because directional continuity errors happen all of the time.

# IS IT REALLY WORKING?
# TIMING AND ANIMATICS

The notion of *timing* may seem a bit abstract at this point. I mean, how can you nail timing on a bunch of static cards? Allow me to explain and emphasize that timing is one of the most important details you'll need to solidify in your storyboarding process. Imagine your horror if you pitch a flawless 30-second motion graphics advertisement to a client only to discover when you sit down to animate that it's two minutes long! There is no amount of charm that can ease you out of that pickle. To avoid such a conundrum, you must work to establish the timing of your project during your storyboarding process.

First step in doing this is to determine how long your whole piece must run, or the Total Running Time (TRT). Now, break your story into three acts and establish how many seconds each act must be. Finally, time each scene, using the dialogue and/or stage direction as a realistic guide. You may find that you have some trimming to do. You might even have to cut some beats that you love very much. Well, time to get brutal because you *must* hit those marks. Once you feel that the timing is worked out, pitch your storyboards again to an audience, this time with a stopwatch in hand.

## The Magic Ingredients: Time and Sound

Still don't trust your timing? It may be time to take a step into the realm of computer animation by creating an *animatic*. An animatic is a video version of your storyboards laid out in sequence on an animation timeline with a soundtrack aligned. It allows you to see your storyboards come to life and get a true sense of how your story will time out.

To create an animatic, you'll need to use a video-editing program. Many are affordable, some even free if you look around: iMovie, Windows Moviemaker, Adobe Premiere, Adobe After Effects, Final Cut, and Toon Boom all work well for creating an animatic. Plus, there's a wealth of YouTube videos that can teach you how to make animatics with any of these programs.

TIME

SOUND

Once you've downloaded the right program, scan and import your storyboards into the program and lay them out on a timeline. If you have recorded dialogue, music, voiceover, or sound effects, import those as well and add them to your sequence. It's going to take some tinkering to get this right, and it will always feel a bit awkward (after all, you are "animating" static shots), but do your best to create an honest timeline of your entire story. You'll need (again) to bring out your most brutal internal editor. If a beat is too long, shorten it. If a beat seems expendable and you need the time, get rid of it. You might even find that you have too much time and be forced to create a new visual beat. Get to work on that immediately and realign your animatic with the new beat. Timing is the truth, and the truth will become crystal clear when you sequence it out on your animatic. This is where surprises and excuses vanish, because the animatic is your last and final chance to get your story right before taking the big leap into animation.

If you feel ready—I mean really ready—then let's go forth!

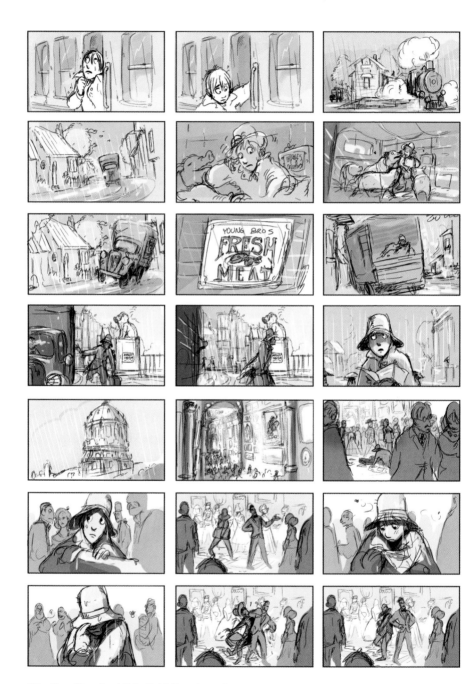

**Sterling Sheehy**, Wakefield Storyboards

# STORYBOARD RECAP

1. **Vary Your Shots Responsibly:** Utilize different-sized shots to enhance narrative logic and drama.
2. **Framing & The Rule of Thirds:** Keep shots interesting by placing subject off-center.
3. **Staging:** Block elements to create visual and conceptual hierarchy.
4. **Spatial Continuity:** Make sure frames are consistent with the physical world you've created.

5. **Temporal Continuity:** Make sure frames are consistent with the story you've been telling.
6. **Directional Continuity:** Make sure things are moving in a consistent direction from frame to frame.
7. **Timing:** Break out a stopwatch and make sure that your story works in the time you've been allotted.
8. **Animatics:** Step into the world of animation by laying out your storyboards into a digital timeline.

## ASSIGNMENT

Storyboard a simple premise

Using the method outlined above, create thumbnails, thumbnail revisions, storyboards, and storyboard revisions for the following simple premise: A character in a bind discovers a magic carpet. Where do they find it? Where do they go? That's all I'm telling you, except that it must be 30 seconds long, exactly. Once you've completed your storyboard, pitch it to a group or a person. Time it out as best you can, and if you can access an editing program, go ahead and lay it into an animatic for final timing.

# 4

# COLOR SENSE
### Enhance your story with the right palette

Color has tremendous storytelling power. It can express emotion, clarify motivation, and even dictate the entire meaning of a piece. A farmer's lush green field means something totally different if instead it's yellow-brown; a hero's ride off into the sunset becomes a ride into the depths of hell with a slight tweak in hue; a young boy's first kiss has a different connotation if the recipient of the kiss turns green instead of blushing red.

So what are the best color choices for your story? What is just the right amount of color to use, if any at all? How can you use color to enhance the emotional impact of your piece? This chapter will answer those questions and give you some simple guidelines for how to plan your palette and enrich your story with well-informed color choices.

**Cody Walzel**, *Makeshift Satellite*, Color Script

# COLOR VOCAB
## *Hue, Saturation, and Value*

First let's make sure we're all on the same page about basic color vocab. As you may know, there are three standard characteristics of color: hue, saturation, and value. When we ask, "What color is that?" we're asking for the hue. *Hue* refers to the common color name in the spectrum like red, blue, green, blue-green, and so on. *Saturation* is the intensity or purity of a color. Highly saturated colors look vibrant and bright while low-saturated colors look dull, almost grayish. *Value* is the relative lightness or darkness of a color—basically how much light the color is exposed to determines its value. Low value means a color is closer to black. I'll use these terms throughout the chapter, so please refer to the hue, saturation, value chart here if you need a refresher.

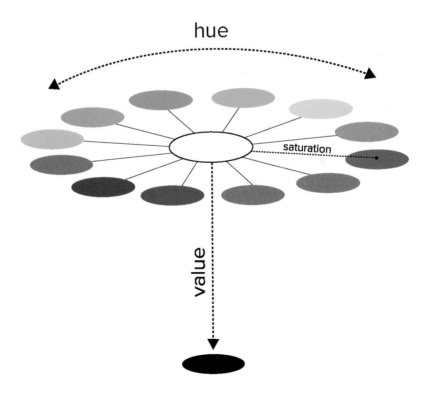

## Create a Color Script

*Let's pull out those cue cards again.* This time, instead of blank ones grab your completed storyboards. If you've already attempted to make an animatic, then your boards likely will be scanned and integrated into an editing program. If not, do so now. Scan each card into the software of your choice and lay out your boards in sequence—it's time to start the process of creating a color script.

A *color script* is a sequential visual outline of how you intend to use color in your animated film. The process can be highly experimental, and, as usual, I encourage you to find a process that works best for you. The trick is to balance what you think looks right in your individual scenes with what helps to enrich your story as a whole. Story is always first, so you may need to replace colors that you absolutely love (aesthetically) if they don't serve the big picture of your story.

To begin, take a step way back and try to define what color your entire story would be if it could be only one color. This is akin to figuring out the theme of your story, as it will influence each of your color choices as you move forward. We'll discuss color symbolism soon, but I encourage you to go with your gut in answering the following questions to help you determine that one color: How does your film feel? Is it a pink film? A gray one? What is the overarching central mood of your film, and is it strong enough to base your film's palette around? Figuring out the dominant, thematic color of your film will help establish the palette of your other colors moving forward.

Once you have that one color, the next step is to create what I call a *pre-color script (PCS)*. This is your storyboard represented by a series of single colors, one for each board. Each color in the series can be repeated. Think of your pre-color script as a game of charades—you have to tell your entire story start to finish but you can use only one color per frame to do so.

The best way to start this process is by identifying the key moments in your story that will require color for emphasis. These are the moments that have to pop in your storyline—and then the color you choose in the rest of your film should act to support those moments as best they can.

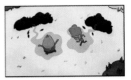

**Louis Morton**, *Nose Hair* Storyboards

Take for instance the story of a bear cub lost in the woods. Say the cub faces off against some dangerous predator during the night and by dawn finally makes her way back home to her family of bears. The moments where color is important seem straightforward: when the bear cub gets lost in the woods, when the cub fights off a dangerous predator, and finally when the cub arrives safely back home. If these key moments are to be represented by solid hues, which would they be?

I encourage you to go with your gut in answering that question, break some rules, and be creative. However, if the ideas aren't flooding in, it doesn't hurt to start your color thinking with popular symbolism that permeates Western culture. Red represents menace, anger, or danger, like Darth Vader's red light saber or Captain Hook's red hat and jacket. For instance, you may think to use a splash of dramatic red when the bear cub is fighting against the violent predator.

Symbolism, however, may not always best serve the scene. What about when our bear cub gets lost in the first place? For the disorientation and fear that the cub may be experiencing, consider changing the value of the existing green so that the whole forest goes a bit darker when the cub realizes that she's lost.

Finally, for the cub's return home, it may be neither hue nor value that best enhances the moment. Perhaps a change in saturation will work best. Through the cub's travels the forest may have become desaturated to imply the sadness of the lost bear cub, but when the cub finally discovers home the forest could return to a saturated green. It will infuse your shot with sudden optimism and joy as the cub runs back towards her family.

Choosing the right hue, saturation, and/or value for the key moments in your story will help to amplify the emotion that you're going for and will also clarify intent. You can assign to a color any meaning you've chosen—you simply have to define and establish it and be consistent with how you use it in your film. Whether you choose Western culture's symbolism or you assign your own meanings, it's important to consider saturation and value as well as hue—and most importantly…go with your gut!

## Supporting Colors

Once you've identified the hue, saturation, and value for the key moments in your story, go ahead and fill in the rest of your scenes with solid colors in the same way. Treat your key moments as the stars and choose colors that act as supporting characters. You may wish to avoid hue, saturation, and value levels that compete for attention with your star's key scenes.

**PRE-COLOR SCRIPT**

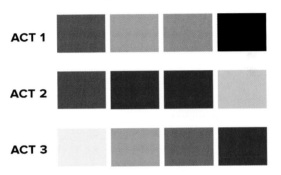

**COLOR SCRIPT**

**Jiali Ma**, *Black Bird*

## Color Me Awesome

Now that you've completed your pre-color script, it's time to move on to the big time and complete your color script. With your PCS as your guide, pull up your original storyboard sequence and begin to work out the colors for each board. The principal color that you already selected will help keep you focused on the look you're going for in each scene. Take the colors that you identified in your PCS and integrate them into the board. Once you do that it's time to select colors for the supporting cast of characters, backgrounds, and props in each shot. Again, I urge you to go with your gut and always consider story above visual awesomeness. And oh...

Remember the important and simple tips I've outlined on the following pages when organizing color for your films. They represent the wisdom of experienced art directors and production designers whose decades of heart-wrenching trial and error led them to see the light. Take heed of their tips, or else their endless suffering will have been all for naught!

**PLEASE NOTE**
In print, colors are created by mixing pigments on paper. Mix too many pigments and you'll get black. In motion, light is used to mix color. If you mix too many colored lights you'll get white. As a result, print and motion function in two different "color systems." Motion uses the additive color system called RGB (Red, Green, Blue). Print uses the subtractive color system known as CMYK (Cyan, Magenta, Yellow, Black). Long story short, if you notice a weird change in your colors when transitioning from print to motion, your files may have changed from RGB to CMYK. Most programs will compensate for this shift, but if things look odd, you may want to go back and change your source files from CMYK to RGB.

Kim Dulaney, *Airbnb*. Lead art direction and design. Character design by Lauren Indovina. Directed by Marco Spier and Marie Hyon. Produced at Psyop

## Tip 1: Limit Your Palette

In still artwork, the eye has time to explore color and investigate composition. With animation (and all film), movement and the passage of time create the need for a continuous and clear focal point. You want your story to read quickly and consistently from scene to scene. Distracting the viewer's eye with unimportant objects that are colorful is the first way to lose the attention of an audience.

Simply put, in choosing color, less is more. Too much color variety in a shot confuses the eye, just as too many flavors on a plate of food will confuse the palate. It's best to take a minimalist approach to color and start with as few colors as possible. It will be far easier to add colors later in the process than to take them away. Limiting your palette will allow the viewer's eye to quickly process the moving images and focus on what is most important in your story.

## Tip 2: Support (Don't Upstage) Your Subject

Be careful with adding too much color to backgrounds and props when you have a colorful moving subject. Moving subjects are your stars and need space to breathe—they should be supported by their surrounding colors, not upstaged.

One way to please your attention-craving star is by designating an open area around it. This area is called a *white space* (though it's not necessarily white). Your subject will thank you for the wide-open stage where they can best be seen, and even if your audience's eye does wander, it will be thankful for a little rest in your white space.

Another way to limit the visual competition around your subject is by using high-contrast or complementary colors. This will help to solidify figure/ground relationships around your subject and will make your subject pop. High contrast is especially important for kinetic type, logos, and broadcast graphics, since words take more time to comprehend than singular objects and therefore require clear figure ground relationships.

**Kim Dulaney**, *Eno*. Lead art direction and design. Directed by Lauren Indovina. Produced at Psyop *(above and opposite page)*

## Tip 3: Select One Thematic and One Accent Color

We went over this during your pre-color script, but I can't stress enough how important it is to choose a dominant thematic color to unify your entire piece. Doing this gives you a basis on which to establish your palette and offers viewers a theme through which they can experience your piece. Once you've established your thematic color, you should focus on selecting an accent color. There are many ways to pick color pairs. Try complementary colors, analogous colors, colors next to each other on the color wheel, whatever. From this dominant and accent color all other color decisions are derived—so choose carefully and choose early.

**Ariel Costa**, *Pixel Show*

**Von Glitschka**, *Tire Goblin*

## Tip 4: Use Saturation Mindfully

Saturated colors are so energetic that they can steal the spotlight if used in the wrong place. Use saturation in important places and moments when you need a character or story point to pop. Rely on it too often and the eye will tire out. In other words, use restraint with saturated colors and save them for when they will help focus the eye and move the story.

## Tip 5: Use Surprise Color for Punctuation

A *surprise* or unexpected color is one that differs so greatly from your overall palette that it jars the eye. When placed at a key moment in your story, a surprise color can enliven your motion work, tie together a key idea, and even trigger the climax of the story. Warning: Much like saturation, surprise colors are very powerful, so use with great restraint.

**Kim Dulaney**, *Linda Loves*. Lead art direction and design. Directed by Jordan Bruner. Produced at Passion Pictures

## Tip 6: Design for Movement

In each of your boards, identify what will be moving and what will remain still. When choosing color, make sure that the colors in your backgrounds and still objects do not compete with the colors in your moving subjects. The goal is to draw the eye towards your subject and to not allow the less important still objects to distract from the action. Think about desaturating the colors in your backgrounds or still objects, and let your star have the spotlight.

## Tip 7: Make Your Own Rules

As you've figured out by now, color is complex. Steadfast rules to using color in motion can be counterproductive to finding the right combination for your film. When it comes to color, uncomfortable combinations and new kinds of usage may make for interesting design. When using color, feel free to make your own rules for a project—just be consistent with them so that your piece is unified.

### COLOR RECAP

Color Vocab: Hue, Saturation, and Value

Make Color Scripts to Emphasize Key Moments

Tip 1: Limit Your Palette

Tip 2: Support (Don't Upstage) Your Subject

Tip 3: Select One Thematic and One Accent Color

Tip 4: Use Saturation Mindfully

Tip 5: Use Surprise Color for Punctuation

Tip 6: Design for Movement

Tip 7: Make Your Own Rules

## ASSIGNMENT
Subvert a nursery rhyme, make a color script

Subvert a simple nursery rhyme by translating it into a film genre, such as horror, comedy, musical, action, sci-fi, or Western. First, write a three-act structure—one sentence per act. Next, select a dominant color for your piece. Then, make a simple pre-color script for your story. If you want a bigger challenge, try storyboarding it in full color!

# WEIRD SCIENCE
## Experiment with animation

*"I call my process Weird Science. It's a mixture of creative rituals and experimentation. We fail a lot and sometimes we're lucky. But if you're doing it right and you're paying attention you begin to learn your own weird science."*
—*Rama Allen, Director, HBO's* True Blood *title sequence.*

Perhaps more than any other film medium, animation provides a breeding ground for experimentation. Not only are your image-making options infinite, but the process allows for wild swings at the bat that perhaps no other medium provides. Experimentation is an essential step in getting the most out of the animated process and may even help you to discover the defining moment in your story. Sometimes stories are even born from the process of animation itself. Still, some skeptics fear the word experimentation—they feel it implies whimsy, which they believe is synonymous with wasting time. If that's how you feel, then please go ahead and replace the word with the more scientific phrase "Research and Development." Because that's what experimentation is. Even the oldest and most sacred techniques and methods can benefit from a fresh round of experimentation.

Take the United States national anthem written in 1814 by Francis Scott Key. The melody was considered sacrosanct when Jimi Hendrix got on stage in 1969 and unleashed a screeching guitar solo before a stunned (if slightly stoned) crowd. It was blasphemy… and yet it was innovative genius. Jimi had taken a tried and true formula for water ($H_2O$) and come up with liquid gold, and "The Star Spangled Banner" would never be the same.

## FIND YOUR WEIRD SCIENCE

Like Rama Allen (quoted previously), Jimi Hendrix made his own weird science to create something new; now it's time for you to find your *weird science*. So steel up your courage, muster up some Hendrix-like chutzpah, and *go there*—mess around, test limits, learn something new that's difficult—or risk leaving behind a crucial element in your animated story. The experimentation of this chapter is designed as a hiatus between the transition from the nitty-gritty of preliminary work of earlier chapters and the technical detail that comes later. What kind of animation magic can you imbue into your project?

Wizard of invention illustrator Ian Wright took a familiar photographic portrait of Jimi Hendrix and through experimentation reinvented it with rolling beads (at right).

**Ian Wright**, *Jimi Hendrix*. Photo by Ed Park *(opposite page)*

## The Importance of Creating "Bad" Art

First step is to create some truly bad art. And since no else will do it, I (The Author) hereby give you (The Artist) permission to make bad art. In fact, I assign you the task of taking at least one scene from your project and making it as bad as you possibly can. Here's what I mean by *bad art*. Forget about careful color choices; go against your instincts with design and technique; get in there and make a mess. Have rain fall upward, layer on effects like icing, turn the grass neon pink. Have fun and commit to trying so many things that you end up with the wildest version of your scene possible. Permit yourself to work on an idea that is meant for no critical eyes ever to see, and I guarantee that you'll learn a ton. You may even decide to incorporate some of your "bad ideas" into the final project. If you do, you may be stunned to discover that audiences react to those bad ideas as some of your best. The reason is simple: When you relax and stop worrying about what people are going to think, you're at your most creative and inventive. When you're at your most inventive, you make the most unexpected creative decisions. And nothing helps enhance a story more than inventive creative decisions. Those moments are the points in your story that people call surprising and magical. And… you never have to let on that those surprisingly magical moments came out of an experimentation with bad art.

## Work on the Edge of Your Skill Set

It was Samuel Beckett who coined the phrase "fail better," and I'm thinking of getting a tattoo that says just that. Trying to improve at things that you genuinely stink at, and not judging yourself for stinking, may be the secret to a fulfilling artistic life. Beckett wasn't being irrational. He didn't want you to flap your arms in an effort to fly or skydive without a parachute. He was talking about working within your area of expertise but just at the edge of your skill set where you get uncomfortable; where from either lack of experience or lack of ability in an area, you stink. Squarely in that zone of that discomfort, right where your stinking is maximus, is where your creative genius will happen. So in your continued effort to create weird science, try going beyond your current comfort zone.

**Jordan Bruner**, *Battista and Federico*

Scores of great artists and directors have become great because they had the courage to be honest about what skills were needed to get to the next level. They didn't wander around trying everything for the sake of it; instead, they were systematic about looking their shortcomings in the eye, turning their backs on the embarrassment and fear of being seen as a fraud, and focusing on expanding their skills. So ask yourself: Where are the gaps in my skill set? What areas of your craft do I feel the need to investigate?

Now, set forth and fill those gaps. Might learning to shoot and edit video sharpen your timing? Need to brush up on character animation? Fascinated but perhaps terrified by motion capture? Take the time to experiment with them—all of them. Ask favors of friends who can show you the basics, take on the persona of a child learning a language who is unafraid of butchering it, and get to work. Caveat: I'm not asking you to perfect what's on that list, just to try it, and lean into the discomfort of not yet being proficient. It's in this uncomfortable process that you may find the key to your artistic greatness and perhaps even crack the secret to failing better.

# PERSONAL EXPERIMENTATION HEAVEN

Up to this point you've permitted yourself to experiment like Jimi Hendrix, make horribly bad art, and learn new skills with the goal of expanding your set. But don't give all that magic to your boss! It's often the unpaid personal projects that will further your craft, keep the creative fires burning, and if you're lucky lead to even bigger things in your career.

## Make the Work You Want to Be Hired to Do

Gregory Herman, multi-disciplinary director and designer who has worked on such blockbusters as *21 Jump Street* and *The Amazing Spider-Man* but also an array of independent film projects, knows a thing or two about getting pigeonholed in Hollywood. When a designer or animator gets known for doing something well, clients come running for specifically that thing. It's easy to get pigeonholed into working on the same kinds of projects over and over. For Herman that thing was broadcast graphics—he composes them brilliantly but isn't totally satisfied doing only one thing. He wants to spend his days expanding his skills and working on a variety of projects that inspire him. Simply put, *he wants to be paid to do the work he wants to do.*

Common sense told Herman that if his reel was filled with broadcast graphics, then he'd end up getting hired to do just that. So he made a strategic choice. He displayed his broadcast graphics work and personal/experimental work side by side on his website and reel. The message to prospective employers was clear: He was a multi-faceted artist, able to do more than just one thing really well.

The *Macro Study* (on the right) is an example of the personal work that Herman spotlighted. *Macro Study* features filmic title sequences with dark, suspenseful soundtracks and close-up images of everyday objects shot with a macro lens. It was the work Herman wanted to do: transforming the seemingly mundane (broken tools, insects, plants, Hot Wheels cars) into mysterious and exciting worlds that tell a new story.

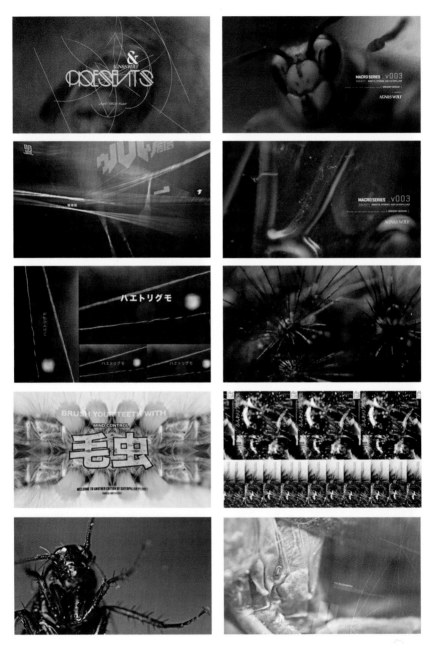

**Gregory Herman**, Director, *Macro Study v003a*

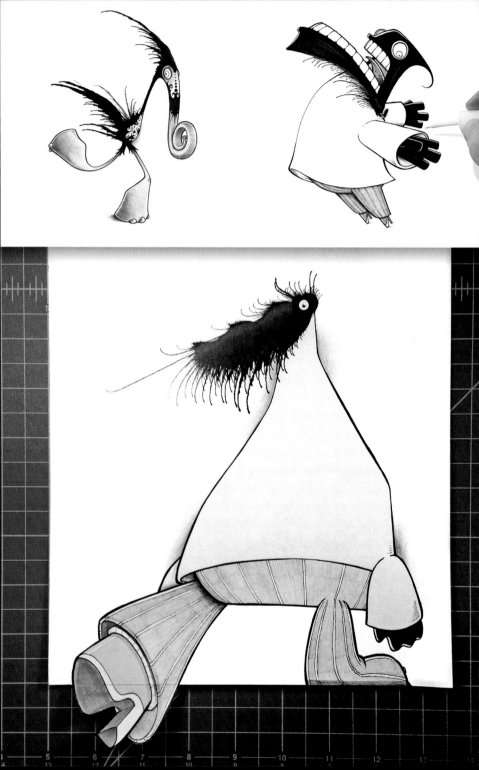

It took some time, but eventually Herman found himself being offered work to create film title sequences just like the ones featured on his site. Not that the graphics work offers dried up; quite the opposite. But now he was allowed to do both and also choose between the work that he had once been pigeonholed to do and the work that really inspired him. The result can be viewed on his impressive website.

## Personal Projects Pay Off in Unexpected Ways

Stefan Bucher is a busy man. A highly sought-after illustrator and designer for top clients, Bucher doesn't have much extra time in his day. And yet, he eked out enough time on the side of his demanding job to create what is likely his most identifiable work. Bucher's *Daily Monster project* began with a simple ink spot on a blank page. He found that blowing air on the ink created an unusual shape, which could form the basis of a kind of magical monster drawing. Bucher became enchanted (and obsessed) with his little ink-faced monster and committed to creating at least one new one a day.

Bucher kept his promise, and soon that single ink spot drawing evolved into over a thousand monster creations. *The Daily Monster project* is now a published book, a popular animated Web series, and (hopefully very soon) a TV show. Bucher carved out precious minutes from his packed daily schedule to follow his bliss, and the payoff has been huge (on the left).

It's the personal projects that will help you identify the stories that you want to tell and further cultivate your point of view. So whether it's keeping an active sketchbook, scribbling down short narratives, or making films on the side, keep the romance alive and find the time to do the work that you want to do. Remember to treat your personal projects with the same professionalism as the work you're getting paid for. You may be surprised at how quickly it gets you noticed, and hired.

**Stefan Bucher**, *Daily Monster 308*

# YOUR FILM'S EXPERIMENTATION LIST

Time to grab a piece of paper and get down to business applying your weird science to your current project. Within each frame of your completed storyboard exists areas that could benefit from experimentation. Draw up a graph with each scene's number on the left side and a series of columns at top listing areas where you might experiment with those scenes. Technique, Design, Movement, Transitions, Sources, and Sound are good examples of areas where you might experiment, but you should add your own columns to best fit the possibilities available in your specific film.

Now that your graph is made, consider how your project as a whole might benefit from each area of experimentation. You may decide that there are many possibilities or just a few. Go through each of your storyboards one by one and consider how you might experiment with each of the topics listed in the column. If you think there's something there, take your best, wildest shot—I assure you it'll be worthwhile.

For inspiration, please remember that sometimes the best way to experiment is not to invent new ways of doing things but to be influenced by something you've seen before and love. Head onto AWN, Motionographer, Vimeo, or YouTube and find something that nails the look you're going for in your own project. Take careful notes of what elements you're responding to and then add these experiments to your list.

## Transitions, A Case Study

Your experimentation list should most certainly include transitions. Animation allows for the most marvelous things to happen in between two frames. Hsinping Pan's film *USOC Henry Cejudo* illustrates how simple design choices can achieve beautiful animated transitions, removing all clunky cuts. Notice in particular how she orchestrates a seamless story transition from the wrestler to his adoring mother by morphing the background of the wrestling stage into his mother's brown eye. We know that the mother is thinking about her son as soon as we see her face without any additional information. The transition became the story.

**Hsinping Pan**, *USOC Henry Cejudo*

## Movement, A Case Study

The word animation is derived from the Latin word "anima," which means soul. How you animate the elements in your piece reveals its soul, so now it's time to get a little James Brown with your project. Do you want certain movement to be smooth and elegant, quirky and comic, or jagged and edgy? Whatever tone you choose and whatever medium you're working in, it's essential to do animation experiments with key characters, assets, and camera moves to feel out which tools work best to get them moving the way you want.

Louis Morton's character movement studies are an elegant example of expressive invented character movement that can only be the result of such experimentation.

**Louis Morton**, *Passer Passer*, Character Movement Studies

**Alberto Scirocco**, leftchannel, *Feed Your Creative Brain*, Motion Conference

## WEIRD SCIENCE RECAP

1. Free yourself to make "bad art."
2. Work on the edge of your skill set.
3. Make the work you want to be hired to do.
4. Keep working on your personal projects.
5. Make a Project Experimentation List.
6. Experiment with transitions.
7. Experiment with movement.

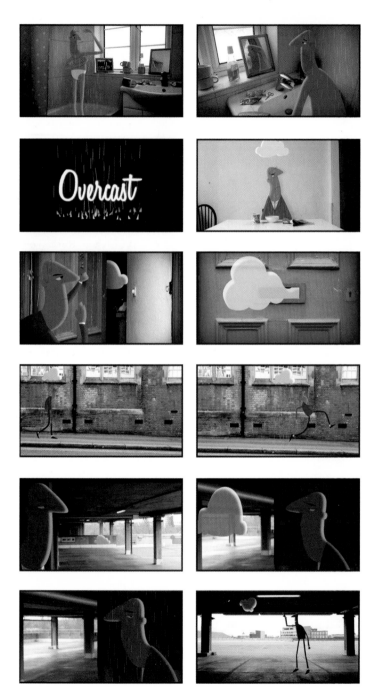

**James Lancett** and **Sean Weston**, Directors, *Overcast*

## ASSIGNMENT
Experiment with non-digital sources

Animation has the ability to take audiences to completely fabricated worlds, but for some content there is a point at which these worlds can feel a bit airless. An audience may need something to ground them, without necessarily leaving the world you created for them. Adding non-digital visual elements and textures from the natural world can help make your film more visually accessible and infuse it with a kind of gritty relateability. And, let's face it, it doesn't hurt to step away from the computer and reconnect with the real world for a minute.

Experiment: Begin a new project or explore one you're already working on for opportunities that might be enhanced by the analog beauty of gritty nature. Gather some visual elements from the real world and integrate them into your animated film. Shoot video; scan paper, textures, or fabrics; take photographs, etc. Be playful with your tools: Whip your camera around to capture weird lights; scan your freckles or a rind of lemon; shoot origami on green screen. Bringing "real-world" warmth and familiarity into your digital environments can infuse your imagined world with a more relatable feeling that can bring a whole new interpretation to your story.

The image at left shows screenshots from the film *Overcast* by James Lancett and Sean Weston. When I spoke to Sean about how he and James decided to mix 2D character animation with real-world video for *Overcast*, he said: "James and I were talking about different techniques of animation dueling with each other. At first, it was CG versus stop motion versus 2D hand drawn…all living in the real world. We soon realized we were putting a bit too much on our plate. So we went along the lines of an out-of-work 2D animated character living in the real world. The story later turned into a depressed character, fed up with his cloud of depression."

*Overcast* is a wondrous example of the visual beauty that can be attained when an animator mixes digital and non-digital sources. But perhaps more importantly, it reveals the way depth can be added to storytelling by combining the worlds. Give it a shot.

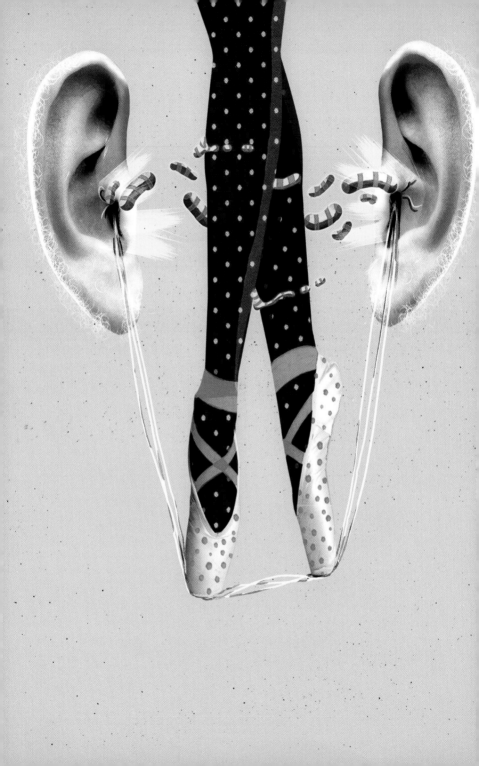

# 6

## SOUND IDEAS
### Get your audio and story in sync

Let's begin with a game of Fill-in-the-Blanks. Lightning strikes and you'll soon hear the sound of _____ . A baby drops his pacifier; plug your ears because here comes _____ . Jay-Z struts onstage in Brooklyn and it's the deafening sound of _____ . The very notion of sound is that it's reactive, almost obedient, to action. Indeed, all sounds are the result of objects vibrating, and so it follows that when creating your animated film, sound should be the result of action and emerge out of existing story. But that conventional wisdom seriously underestimates the enormous power of sound not only to affect current story but also to propel it forward on its own. You have only to catch an episode of Looney Tunes with Bugs Bunny to witness the indelible power of sound. Bugs is chased into a dark bear cave by Yosemite

Sam and the screen goes completely black. You hear scuffling, punches, and groans. Then in the next frame Bugs strolls out of the cave, carrot in mouth, unscathed, and grinning smugly—but the fighting sounds persist. We viewers all know that Yosemite Sam is still in that cave, very likely fistfighting with an angry bear, and it ain't gonna end well…

It's a nice example of how sound alone can paint a vivid picture of action and can propel story forward on a blank screen. But that's just a warm-up. Consider the figure below. A man's terrified face—eyes wide like saucers. Let's add the eerie sound of screeching violins, heavy footsteps, then the creaking of a door and cocking of a handgun—a murderer has clearly arrived and death is only seconds away. Same image; add mushy romantic music, the sound of young ladies giggling, and high-heeled footsteps followed by the voice of a shy young woman, "Hello, Harold, you look soooo handsome in your bowtie and suspenders." Suddenly, our man is far from being murdered but is instead totally love-struck, on the verge of a blushing meltdown. Finally, change the soundtrack again to a buzzing alarm clock, the distant sound of morning traffic, and a dog whining and wagging his tail against a bedside (ready for his morning walk). Suddenly our almost-murdered love-struck man is none of those things—he has simply overslept and is late for work!

# LET SOUND LEAD STORY

In production, sound can be an afterthought, but waiting until the middle (or after) animation to determine your soundtrack is kind of like waiting until there's a minute left in the fourth quarter of a pick-up game to sub in LeBron James. Talk about a missed opportunity! I challenge you to not only consider your soundtrack at the same time as writing and design in your production timeline but to *lead with sound*, using it as the primary compass for your storytelling. You may be surprised at its Zeus-like story power (*as lightening follows the sound of thunder!*), and your project will glow from that uniquely ear-forward approach.

## Diegetic and Non-diegetic Sound

Karin Fong, award-winning founder of Imaginary Forces and acclaimed title designer, is fond of saying that music and audio "does 80 percent of the work." I'm not going to promise that this chapter will help you complete 80 percent of your project, but if you follow the strategies laid out in this chapter I can guarantee that your story will be stronger as a result.

First we need to clarify the concept of "diegetic" and "non-diegetic" sound (pronounced *daya-jet-ic*). Put simply, *diegetic sound* comes from sources that are visible on-screen (or implied by action off-screen) and that come from the physical world: a dog's bark, a creaking door, most dialogue (that is not in the head of a character), and music whose source you can see in the scene—such as from a musician or a radio.

Sounds described as *non-diegetic* are sounds whose source neither is visible on the screen nor has been implied to be present in the action. Sound effects that are not natural to objects in the scene (a sad trombone playing "wah-wah-wah" when a character realizes they've been tricked), the music score (that is not coming from a musician or a radio in the scene), and any off-camera narration or dialogue that's going on in the mind of a character. Non-diegetic sound is *surreal* to the action and yet aims to enrich what is happening on-screen.

# DIEGETIC VS. NON-DIEGETIC SOUND

| DIEGETIC (LITERAL) | NON-DIEGETIC (NON-LITERAL) |
|---|---|
| **EXAMPLES:** | |
| dialogue — actors speaking | |
| sound effects — door creaking, phone ringing | **EXPRESSIVE SURREAL** |
| music coming from a sound sytem or played in the scene | **EXAMPLES:** |
| **NATURALISTIC REAL** | narration / voice over |
| | sound effects used expressively |
| | music score |
| Sound source visible: implied by action on or off screen, sound coming from the physical world of the film. | Sound source not visible or connected to narrative universe of film. |

Animation offers a host of opportunities to use both diegetic and non-diegetic sound and also provides many occasions where one can morph into the other. For instance, a baby is crying loudly. Those cries are diegetic—you can see the baby and know that they're upset, even as the crying grows loud enough to break a glass. What if you add a surreal emphasis to that baby's cry and make it grow louder and more ferocious and morph it into the mighty roar of a lion or the howl of an ambulance siren? Now you've augmented the story; the baby's cry is so loud and ferocious it sounds like a lion to those around it, and it only took a simple swap from diegetic to non-diegetic sound.

Below we'll explore the three elements of sound in animation and motion graphics—sound effects, music, and dialogue—with an ear for both diegetic and non-diegetic sound. The chart above reminds you of the choices you have when creating a soundtrack for your film: from totally naturalistic diegetic (baby's cry/band playing/dialogue) to surreal non-diegetic (lion's roar from a baby's mouth/music soundtrack/narration and internal monologue) to everything in between. The medium of animation celebrates creative flexibility when it comes to sound, so take advantage!

## Sound Effects

Adding sound effects to your project can be a blast. Who can resist the howl of a werewolf when a terrified character is walking alone in the woods at night? What good is a brilliant idea without a "ding!" for emphasis? What editor hasn't toyed with the plethora of burping cues available at a keystroke to enhance a post-soda drinking scene? With so many delicious possibilities at your fingertips, *restraint is key*. Indeed, the first step in adding sound effects to your film is to make a list of places where you'd like to add them and slash that list in half (at the very least!). While well-placed sound effects enhance your story, their overuse will leave a film suffering from the law of diminishing returns. Take the much-loved *cymbal* used to heighten dramatic moments in-scene. A verbal sparring between two slugs can be clattered with cymbals in an effort to elevate the drama, and it might work nicely for a while. But what happens when one slug gets so angry that it pulls out a *deadly saltshaker?* Adding another heightened cymbal will have lost its emphasis and will come off as limp, white noise.

A proficient user of sound effects is quite the poet: They require great restraint but also a knack for metaphor and a love of the surreal. After all, what are sound effects but lyrical dips into the universe of the fantastic? The sight of children playing in the street touches a grumpy old man, and the sound of a "cracking iceberg" may represent the melting of his frozen heart. A corrupt politician is caught red-handed committing evil in full public view, while the sound of sirens and helicopters circling may embody the feeling that there is no escape. A woman is struck by cupid's arrow, and chirping birds may best represent her feelings of romantic affection—or maybe her heart *literally sings* ABBA? AC/DC? Pavarotti? Whatever the scenario or your take on that metaphor, when you are tempted to use a naturalistic (diegetic) sound, first search your poet's soul for a surreal sound that might embody what you're trying to express. It may just capture the emotion you're reaching for in a more expressive way, and your audience will appreciate that poetic reach.

## Music as sound effects

So you've got your trimmed list of sound effects and the perfect metaphors for those opportunities—you are, in fact, ready to receive your Pulitzer Prize for Poetry. But before you deliver your acceptance speech, consider that some of your sound effects might not have to be "effects" at all. They could in some cases be more effective as music, especially music derived from the soundtrack that you've created for your film (which we discuss next). Classic examples of using sound effects derived from soundtrack are the famous screeching violin in Hitchcock's *Psycho* shower scene; the ominous piano *dun-dun* from Spielberg's *Jaws* when the mega-shark approaches; the playful sound of a piccolo in the classic cartoon *Tom & Jerry* when the mouse evades the cat with his quick little footsteps. Borrowing sound effects from your music score is a great move since it can give your effects an organic feel, while also giving your entire soundtrack the feeling of synthesis—not an easy task when selecting sounds for an entire animated film.

**NOTE ON FOLEY SOUND**

Scores of sound effects libraries can be accessed online for free or for a small purchase, and the choices may seem overwhelming. But I implore you: Do not depend on someone else's sound to express your story ideas. You can make your own sounds that are more specific to your vision with a simple microphone setup. Recording your own Foley sound effects allows you to create the exact sounds that you hear in your head and not settle for a near-match. Foley sound is your sound, so why leave such an important aspect of your project in the hands of someone else?

# Music

We all know how important a well-thought-out music score is to the success of your project. More than any other aspect of film, music can determine the emotional tenor of story, set rhythm for scenes, and guide an audience's journey. Luckily, music is malleable. You can orchestrate it so elegantly with your story that audiences may barely even notice it's there. Or you can put it front and center to announce the mood changes and express the overall attitude of your piece. What would *Shaft* be without Isaac Hayes' funky anthem? Where would *Fantasia's* dancing brooms be without Tchaikovsky's *Sorcerer's Apprentice*? Who is Darth Vader without the famously ominous soundtrack that accompanies him into every room?

So let's get down to brass tacks and establish some tools for using music to enhance story in your animated project. Warning: Follow these tools and you may need a ten-piece funk band to blast your theme song whenever you walk into a screening of your film...

## Score to "theme"

Head way back to Chapter 1 of this book ("Pre-production") where you identified the theme and emotional tenor of your project. Now, if you could choose one song that encompasses that theme and emotion, what would it sound like? A triumphant rock song? Lonely blues number? Chaotic free jazz jam a la Ornette Coleman? Find that song (or create it) to style the thematic basis of your music soundtrack. This stage is called building a temp (temporary) track. Be warned, don't get married to music you can't get the rights to. The purpose here is to establish the feeling you're looking for. Use that track as a guide to dig in for other songs that might represent the emotion of various scenes in your project. If you chose lonely blues as your theme, dig out that happy B.B. King song for when your character is finally cured of his/her loneliness. Next, look for tracks that best represent your main characters, as well as for situations that may be repeated in your storyline. These songs will help you define the theme and tone you set out to achieve, and should inspire you to create or acquire final songs that you can get rights to.

## Consider the music of "silence"

I'm not just talking about eliminating music altogether. Certainly, you should always ask yourself if a scene needs music and then leave it bare if the answer is no. Less is more when it comes to music. But there is a kind of music soundtrack that can feel like no music at all to the audience while still providing a powerful emotional push to a scene. Atmospheric music, sometimes represented by a stripped-down hum from your soundtrack or a subtle rhythmic drone, can give a scene added personality that the audience may not even perceive. The primary advantage of using this *quiet* music is that it feels like a breather for the audience, a time during which they can experience your story on their own, while still giving them the slightest nudge into your intended direction. Good sound design is said to be undetectable, and silent music provides the perfect opportunity to integrate your soundtrack seamlessly while still elevating your emotional environment.

## Score against

Perhaps the most horrific scene I have ever witnessed is in Quentin Tarantino's classic film *Reservoir Dogs*. A hit man is about to cut off the ear of a man he believes to be a police informant. It's a brutally violent moment, and any other filmmaker would have thrown in a gruesome soundtrack to match. But Tarantino, in an intentional stroke of genius that epitomizes *scoring against* the action in a scene, has the hit man flip on the radio from where the whimsical 70s pop song "Stuck in the Middle with You" blasts out. The hit man joyfully skips around the informant he plans to disfigure to the upbeat tune, which makes the whole experience so much more disturbing. This kind of contrasting music choice places the audience in an uncomfortable spot and alerts them that something totally off-kilter is happening, so keep your eyes wide open. Just make sure, like Tarantino did, that you pay off that promise when you signal its arrival. Though, there's no need to lose an ear over it…

# Dialogue

Time to summon story guru Robert McKee with this little gem from his seminal work *Story*: "The best advice for writing film dialogue is don't." As an animator, you're creating a project in the most visually dexterous art form in existence; if you can't find a way to express a thought visually, then you haven't tried hard enough. However, if you have exhausted all else and *must* use dialogue (admittedly, I'm a sucker for some good dialogue), here are a few steps you can take to make sure it's awesome.

First step is to match every line of dialogue to the personality of the character you have speaking it. Each line should aim to further reinforce the traits you've given them and clarify those traits for your audience. If a super-egotistical wizard is asked her profession, "I am a wizard" seems like a missed opportunity. How about: "Google me," or "I've already sewed the answer to that question onto the inside of your trousers." Once your script is complete, you should be able to cover up the character headings and read through knowing exactly which character is saying which line since only they could possibly say something so very "them."

Second consideration when writing dialogue is to make your characters speak in as naturalistic a way as possible. In real life people interrupt, veer off into odd directions, use slang and malapropisms constantly. Rarely when a man comes home after a hard day's work is "Hi, Honey, I'm home" his first utterance. Nor does his spouse (in the real world) say "Welcome home, Darling, let me take your coat." More likely he sighs loudly as he kicks off his shoes, muttering bitterly about a late train, after which his annoyed spouse says, "Leftover pizza in the fridge. We couldn't wait. Oh, and your mother called again. She wants to visit."

One surefire way to keep dialogue naturalistic is to indulge in the fine art of subtext in your dialogue—text with a suggested, subtle meaning. People use it all the time, it can be very funny if used right, and (more importantly) dialogue with subtext forces the audience to follow your story more attentively. In a scene where one space alien (Zork) is jealously competitive with a neighbor, you don't want him to say, "My X-5 space cruiser is far larger and more impressive than yours!" Better that Zork leans over the hedges, eyes the other alien's (Gaxx) smaller vehicle and grins, "Cute space cruiser." Gaxx, who is equally competitive, may reply, "Almost bought the X-5, but it's known as the cruiser divorced men buy to over-compensate for size." Subtext is delicious to use, it tends to loosen up dialogue that feels too on the nose, and it gives the audience fun play-along where they have to figure out what's really being said. It's a more interactive and clever way to write.

Finally, use dialogue to set the mood of your scenes. In a tense moment, people tend to speak in shorter, clipped sentences. Says the bouncer to a couple of thugs, "Out. Both of you. Now." In more lighthearted moments, people tend to speak in an almost musical way, often going overboard with details. "We were out all night, and you know Henry, he's so loud, screaming, 'It's my birthday, It's my birthday,' the neighbors we're pounding on the wall and he kept yelling at the top of his lungs, none of us could stop him, so I just gave in to the chaos. Mitch laughed so hard he spit out his birthday cake!"

FYI, if you're writing internal monologue, these guidelines are just as important. The inside of your character's brain is a character, too, and it needs all the personality-driven naturalistic traits that all characters do.

## NARRATION/VOICEOVER FOR MOTION GRAPHICS

While in character-based animation you can choose whether or not to lock your sound script before animating, in motion graphics, where a client often has a specific TRT (Total Running Time) for you to hit, there is no choice: You must lock script and lay down audio before animation begins. It's for that reason that when writing a motion graphics script your best friends are clarity and brevity. Your script must be so simple that there is no room for misinterpretation, and brief enough (given the time limit) that there should exist no words except those absolutely necessary to getting your point across.

**Richard E. Cytowic.** TED-Ed Lessons Worth Sharing, *What percent of your brain do you use?*

That may sound relatively easy, but there's an additional juggling act to pull off: While crafting your written message you must be simultaneously conceptualizing the images and the sequences that you think will best match your words. This mental storyboarding is the key to writing narration that will work in the final edit of your piece. So write brief and write clear, but also write visual.

After a final-locked draft is written, it should be performed and edited multiple times to get a sense of how it's timing out and where the natural rhythm of the piece is going. You may find that it needs to be slowed down, and lines need to be modified and removed to stay within your time length. Testing it out will also provide clues to where effects and music naturally fall.

Once your script is recorded (tight as a bear trap and clear as the bluest sky), you should move on to determine what music might be playing before, during, and after the narration. Per the music section of this chapter, you know how important music is to tone and rhythm, and the music should complement not compete with the narrator's voice. At the latest Motionographer F5 conference, director and designer Patrick Clair said about informational motion graphics, "The pace of the voice drives things, type sits at the center, and design is the spoonful of sugar that helps the medicine go down...."

Finally, it's time to move on to design and animation. There are infinite ways to go about designing your animation to support your copy. Ask yourself how typography, icons, characters, photographs, and video may fit to best tell your story. TED-Ed has created over 120,000 beautiful, fascinating, educational short animated films this way. The TED-Ed animated lesson on the previous page shows how important it is to keep images clean and simple to support scientific content. As always, the big idea and message will determine the media you choose and how it will look. For more inspiration, check them out online at ed.ted.com.

# A FINAL WORD ON TIMING

As they say in comedy, "Timing is everything," and it's just as true in animation. None of what you've just learned—whether it be about effects, music, or dialogue—will work without a keen eye on timing. You will quickly learn that placing a sound effect or music cue a few frames off could be the difference between an emotionally satisfying sound and one that distracts or works against what you were going for. With each cue, sound effect, or bit of dialogue, carefully consider if its placement packs the maximum emotional punch. Often a nudge in one direction or another can provide that beautiful rush of dopamine to the brain that really means, Wow, nice use of sound!

## SOUND IDEAS RECAP

1. Let sound lead story
2. Diegetic and non-diegetic sound
3. Sound effects
4. Music as sound effects
5. Music
6. Dialogue
7. Narration/Voiceover
8. Timing is everything...

## ASSIGNMENT
Experiment with sound

Select a significant moment from a sequence in one of your stories, or find a scene to download. Storyboard it out in detail and import your frames to a video-editing program. Experiment with at least five different music cues that emphasize distinctive emotional tones for the story beat. Don't forget to try scoring against story with unexpected music. Now do the same with sound effects, looking for different ways to make the moment in your scene resonate.

# 7

# DESIGN WONDERLAND
## World building and environmental design

Improv comedy has a golden rule that can be summed up in two simple words: "Yes, and." *Yes, and* means that no matter how ridiculous an idea one player introduces into a comedic scene, the others must accept it as fact and even expand on its authenticity. So if a spastic improv player points to the sky and says, "Look, a giant carrot!" the other players on stage must immediately react. The giant carrot simply exists in this world the moment it's introduced, and unless someone else introduces the idea that gravity works differently, then the giant carrot in the sky is very likely careening down towards them. If a player doesn't jump out of the way they'll be crushed. If they're crushed the surviving players should look down at their dead friend and mourn; or run away worried that another giant falling carrot may be on its way; or feel peckish and decide to dine on a delicious carrot snack.

Animation allows you to create any crazy chaos you want (including giant falling carrots), and, as you've seen in previous chapters, that's just part of the medium's magic. Audiences will be eager to explore whatever bizarre, new environments you create. But once you introduce your world (and all of its strange rules), you must commit to them fully or risk losing that audience forever. Your human character has lost her glasses in a world of Cyclops? Make sure it's very difficult for her to find a new pair since the opticians sell only monocles. Created an environment that is completely upside down? Sleeping bats should stand upright. Families live in marshmallow houses? There should be a slight bounce in their steps on the way to the kitchen.

Committing the sin of going against the wild logic of your world means "continuity issues," and that is the quickest road to having your story lose credibility. Says award-winning filmmaker and educator Brooke Keesling, "Continuity issues are a major pitfall of creating new environments in animation, so artists have to be extra careful to stick to the rules they have created. This is especially important in big story moments—it's critical that story agree with the rules you've set up."

The audience will follow whatever wackiness you throw at them, and they'll take it very seriously so long as they feel that you're doing the same. But one slip, one tiny continuity *oops…* and it's over; your audience will lose interest and *vamoose*. So when your giant falling carrot appears, jump!

## DESIGNING THE RULES

So how do you create an interesting, consistent, and believable animated world? What is the best method for making it feel authentic even as you're turning logic upside down? First, establish time and place, and then do the work to define the physical, social, and visual laws that exist there. These "laws" will provide a consistent foundation for whatever far-flung chaos you envision and will help give your world a sense of authenticity and verisimilitude. So, let's get to work.

**Sirirat Yoom Thawilvejakul**, *Into Mister Sharky's Mouth*

## Your World's Time and Place

Animated environments can range from real-world settings to a mixture of reality and fantasy to full-on fantasy. Whatever direction you choose, you'll need to give your audience a clear sense of time and place. When defining what era your world may exist in, think carefully about technology and other factors that may vary greatly across the decades. Choose the time and the place that will help create the best story, and fill your environment with details that will facilitate interesting conflicts in your story.

Take the story of a heartsick bug that's too shy to express his feelings to a lady bug who is leaving town. If your environment is designed to be like the underground tunnels of an ant colony (set a hundred years in the future), then your pining protagonist will have a hard time finding the right tunnel to catch to the "super-fast flying space bus" that his true love has just boarded. The details of time and place work to elevate the story's conflict—the love-struck bug must express his feelings to the lady bug—but your world is providing an organic roadblock.

**Cody Walzel**, *Breadheads* concept art

Time and place are the first important decisions you'll make in creating your story wonderland. Choose well since that decision provides the backbone of the world where the important physical, social, and visual laws are to be established.

## Your World's Physical Laws

On Earth there are certain indisputable physical laws that are so much a part of our daily lives that we take them for granted. A brick will fall faster than a feather; a pot of water will boil at 212 degrees Fahrenheit; the sun will always rise from the east; and so on. I encourage you to study these physical laws—they will not only help you understand how things work in our environment, but they'll provide you with a reference to turn Earth's physical laws directly on their head when your time comes to do so. Sure, water freezes at 32 degrees Fahrenheit on this boring planet, but what if your world exists between the hair follicles of a mystical beast; or floats in a distant galaxy; or is wedged between the crusts of a tuna sandwich eaten by ancient gods? At what temperature would you have water freeze in those scenarios? And (just as importantly) is it even worth you considering a change in that particular physical law at all? The answer to that question rests on whether or not creating a new physical law will enhance or detract from your story. Put plainly: *Don't just do it because it seems cool. Do it because it's meaningful to the telling of your story.*

Warns Brooke Keesling, "Be careful with overly busy or overly described environments unless they are contributing to the story. Sometimes an environment is the star, or kind of the key character, and sometimes it is just distracting. Even the most amazingly inventive environments can ruin a story if they compete with the main characters and diffuse the key ideas of the story."

**Sterling Sheehy**, Concept Art

**Sterling Sheehy,** *Dragon* Concept Art

## Your World's Social Laws

On Earth, a bunch of men (and sometimes women) got together and made up a bunch of rules for civilized society to follow. A lot of the laws are based on religious values and are aimed at helping the rich rather than the poor (…but, that's just one animator's opinion!). So why not create a new set of social laws and norms for your world? Why not shake things up so long as it aids in the telling of your story? Maybe babies have all the political power; perhaps instead of jail time all criminals must bake giant cupcakes; school is now recess and kids run outside at break excited to study math; dogs walk obedient humans before heading off to work.

Much like with Earth's physical laws, I encourage you to dig into Earth's history—a bunch of mind-bending social norms have existed in various places in the world that may provide you with inspiration for your invented world. Barring the existence of those norms you'd like to keep, the sky's the limit! Make life better or worse, or stranger even, for its inhabitants, and take advantage of how those new social norms can enhance your story.

Take our lovelorn bug who has finally caught up with the lady bug of his dreams and poured his heart out. Romantic comedies usually call it a day there—the lady bug will either reject his proposal or fall into his many arms and buzz off into happily ever after. But why end there if your world has a different set of social laws? Perhaps in your world a lady bug only accepts a proposal once a male bug performs an Elvis impersonation of "Don't Be Cruel." Or let's flip gender roles and say that in your world only lady bugs can propose and it's the male bug who has to first catch the bus and then convince the lady bug to propose! Sure, Elvis-only proposals seem weird, but no weirder than the act of humans bending on their knees and presenting a piece of jewelry.

## Be inspired by nature

If you require inspiration, look no further than our super-freaky natural world. Did you know that there's a bird called the red-capped manakin whose mating ritual includes the male having to perform a backwards dance (much like the moonwalk) before she accepts him? And the male hooded seal attracts mates by inflating a "nasal balloon" into a pink bubble gum-like bulb up to the size of a bowling ball (gross!). For the praying mantis, it gets straight up cannibalistic: After mating, the female mantis generally begins consuming the male alive!

The world we live in is plenty odd when it comes to social norms, and for the most part we follow along like sheep! So why not invent your own set of laws and set your characters free to experience them? You'll be surprised what kind of lunacy your audience will follow along with as long as you remain consistent. So look that audience straight in the eye and say, "This is how it goes around here, so better brush up on your Elvis."

## Your World's Visual Laws

The success of your animated story depends on the tone set by your visual world. Space, line, shape, color, contrast, and texture are all visual aspects you can create laws for as a means to enhance your narrative and distinguish your story from others.

Perhaps our lovesick bugs are a kind of firefly that lights up only when they're with their true love and therefore the film becomes bright and colorful when they're together. Or maybe you're creating a futuristic world run by evil smartphones? You might decide to use desaturated colors, limit the use of any organic forms, and use mostly hard edges and geometric shapes to reinforce a robot-controlled environment. Doing a mysterious detective story? Perhaps limit your palette to black, white, and grays with small pops of color when clues are revealed. Maybe the shots in the detective's office are composed of only right angles to show the detective is in control, while out in the field the shots are composed of only diagonal lines to communicate that he has lost control. Consistent and mindful visual choices made when designing your environment will strengthen your story. So make a list of ground rules and stick with your vision. Audiences will appreciate the fresh take and may even laud this *unique* style. Feel free to tell them that you were inspired by the poetry of Beaudeliere and not that you nerdily taped your visual law list to your computer. Up to you!

## ON MOTION GRAPHICS AND BRANDING

Since most motion graphics use uniquely branded products, identities, or logos in place of easily identifiable human or animal characters, it's even more important to create distinct visual laws to capture an audience's attention. Brands are products, services, and offerings that are organic, breathing entities. Once you've studied the core values of the brand, you can begin to design a world around it.

Kim Dulaney's award-winning opening title sequences (at right) for the OFFF International Festival for the Post-Digital Creation Culture is a rich and elegant world built around a very interesting brand and some very interesting ideas. Dulaney explains, "The concept was to find a balance between nature and machine, along with forms in nature that symbolized strength." The video interestingly explores peculiar spaces fusing the natural and artificial and features hybrid animals that after close inspection reveal wires. In the end, the audience is unable to discern what is animal or machine, natural or synthetic. This elegantly expresses the values and ideas of the OFFF organization.

**Kim Dulaney,** Lead art director, designer, and illustrator. OFFF Online Flash Film Festival title. Creative direction by Jeff Stevens. Produced at The Mill

## DESIGN WONDERLAND RECAP

1. Design consistent rules
2. Define time and place
3. Consider physical laws
4. Consider social laws
5. Define visual laws
6. Motion graphics—explore brand values
7. Motion graphics—establish visual rules

## ASSIGNMENT
### Design and test your new world

Following the items listed in Fictional World Building (at right), establish the rules of a fictional world. Once you've designed your world, I encourage you to throw in some conflict that will act as a stress test for the rules of your world.

Unleash a flying baby or a giant spider; make everyone billionaires; throw in a lunatic with a gun that shoots bubble gum and everyone is covered in mounds of chewing gum! Throw yourself multiple curve balls to test the laws of your own creation. If the laws still hold up after that, you're good!

Note: As you're establishing rules for your world, you may want to do some sketches. This is where storytelling, scriptwriting, and design should come together seamlessly. Since the magic and rules of the physical world are often where interesting conflicts come from, you may need to go back and forth between design and writing to get your world feeling right.

# ⋮FICTIONAL WORLD BUILDING⋮

**1.** What is the place and time of your world? Is your world under water? In space? A totally invented place? Does this world take place in the past, the present, or the future?

**2.** What are the physical rules of this world? Is there gravity? What is necessary for survival? Is all air safe to breathe?

**3.** What are the societal rules of this world? Laws? Punishments? Who has power? What does the society value and believe in?

**4.** What is day-to-day life like in your new world? Where do your characters...Live? Work? Eat? Play? Go to school?

**5.** What is their technology? Transportation? Communications?

**6.** What do their family structures look like? Are there other communities? Other species?

**7.** What interesting conflicts can arise from the rules and environment you've built?

# 8

# TECHNIQUE
## Marry style and story

Here we are at the final stop before animation begins! I'll bet you can almost feel those pixels dancing as your baby finally comes to life. Far be it from me to slow a moving train, but it's my duty to ask one last question here, one that I urge you to consider very carefully: *Have you chosen the best animation technique to tell your story?*

I know, you love 3D; you're a whiz at After Effects (and have a shelf full of awards to prove it); your hand-drawn animation is unparalleled; and so on. It can be difficult to deviate from your best-known and loved technique, and it's easy to convince yourself that your most-practiced technique is the only way to tell your story. Animators tend to get especially defensive when the notion of using a technique they don't already know rears its ugly head. "After all that work, you want me to learn WHAT?!"

Not exactly what I'm asking. I simply don't want you to overlook an essential decision regarding a crucial element of visual storytelling because you don't know some silly computer program. Selecting the right animation technique can be the key to expressing your big idea, can amplify the very soul of your story, and if used inventively can set your project apart from the rest. It should be noted that there are many successful animators and storytellers who spend their career mastering and expressing themselves with one technique. The key here is that they choose to tell the kinds of stories that are best suited for that specific technique.

Consider what Apple's iPod commercials (2003) would have been without pared-down 2D motion graphics or Chipotle's film-turned-advertisement *Back to the Start* (2011) without the innocent and charming 3D stop motion? Is it even possible to imagine Hayao Miyazaki masterful films articulated in a different technique than hand drawn?

Successful directors belabor over which techniques they use in each project, and so should you. Choose wrong and your film may feel like you're driving with square wheels; choose right and you're gliding down the freeway.

## FINDING A PERFECT MATCH

Later in the chapter we'll explore how to adapt your favorite animation technique to capture the essence of a technique that might better suit your story. But for now let's tackle the big question by re-exploring your narrative and also taking a look at how content is viewed today.

### Consider Format

First thing to consider when choosing an animation technique is how it will be viewed. This used to be pretty simple—a film was enjoyed in theaters or commercials were watched on TV. But technology is changing by the minute, making scale a critical and evolving consideration. Certainly, more and more content is being viewed on small computer screens, tablets, phones, and even (gasp!) watches. You should be ready for the very real possibility that your big-screen masterpiece will be enjoyed on a smartphone, so you'd better choose a technique that is legible on that format.

At the same time, some formats are getting much bigger. Film festivals and advertisers are video-mapping on the sides of buildings, screens are beginning to cover billboards and complexes in urban areas everywhere, and "sky-screens" as big as 1,500 feet are popping up in shopping malls from Vegas to Beijing. On these super-sized formats you'll see far more texture and detail, so your technique had better stand up to a magnifying glass.

In the end, you must choose your technique to suit the format you believe it will be viewed on by most people. Choose poorly and risk audiences missing important elements of your story, or even spotting flaws in your work. Pay heed to format, and your project will be seen the way you intended: as an expression of your hard work and talent.

**PLEASE NOTE**
For smaller formats, "vector" graphics and 2D animation with higher contrast read well. They are clean and clear and excellent for communicating information. For extra-large formats, you can choose from a variety of techniques, but keep in mind that your design will be blown up exponentially (an eyelash could end up being several stories high!). So use lots of detail and texture to keep all that screen space interesting.

## Translate Your Story

The most important consideration when choosing an animation technique for your film is all about story. You want to find the tools that strike at your story's metaphoric core by staying true to the message and the tone. You may want to head back to your *creative brief* (see Chapter 1 "Pre-production") to remind yourself of how you want audiences to describe your project when all is said and done. For example, if you're going for something comedic with the feel of a parody, you want to choose a technique that has built-in irony. Stop motion, or its digital counterpart After Effects, works well for offbeat comedy. You may want to avoid techniques that can come off as moody or too naturalistic, like hand-drawn or 3D CGI (computer-generated imagery).

The now iconic *Mad Men* opening titles used a mixture of techniques that so nailed its tone and message that it seems almost inevitable. The creators wanted to express the complex, desolate world of New York City advertising, both glamorous and isolating. Using flat 2D silhouettes of a falling man, they achieved an ominous, noir mood. The falling man appears against shiny buildings covered in perfect plastic advertising photos from the 60s and captures the dichotomy of Don Draper's world: idealized appearances versus stark emotional despair. The design is minimalist and sparse, short on detail so that the eye focuses on the falling man. Certainly, the sequence would have felt too far removed from reality if a hand-drawn technique had been utilized, and the world would have been too singularly slick with only 3D CGI. The creators picked just the right techniques to fit their story, and so can you.

Below is a list of techniques and styles you may consider for your project and a description of how they can enhance your storytelling. Feel free to choose more than one, since a partnership (like in *Mad Men*) may be the best choice.

# ANIMATION/MOTION GRAPHIC TECHNIQUES + STYLES

## Hand Drawn

Hand-drawn animation can be executed with a variety of materials (such as pencil, paint, ink, and charcoal), with styles that range from traditional Disney cel animation to rotoscoping (tracing live-action) to a more fine art hand-drawn approach. Purposely looser hand-drawn styles are frequently seen in independent films (see Don Hertzfeldt, Frédéric Back, Julia Pott) and lend themselves to more expressive, emotionally driven stories. Cel animation, meanwhile, can achieve a clean, almost commercial feel that works especially well for children's entertainment.

## Stop Motion

Stop motion animation has both 2D and 3D versions—similar in technique but different in how they're shot. Both are captured with a camera, shooting frame-by-frame, while objects are moved incrementally in between the frames. The limited motion that results gives stop motion films a quirky and magical quality that is still very popular today despite the availability of more advanced technology.

2D stop motion is shot with a camera held over a flat surface (light boxes are often used for sand, oil, paint, or paper silhouettes). This technique gives a flat, handmade quality to films that is emotionally expressive and very adaptable. 2D animation with paper cutouts can feel quirky and comedic (see Terry Gilliam's *Monty Python*) but also elegant and dream-like (see Lotte Reiniger's silhouette puppets). 2D stop motion with sand or paint can feel lush, moody, and atmospheric (see Caroline Leaf's *The Street*). 2D stop motion technique tends to have a lot of personality and works well if you want your film to have a flat, handmade quality. Please note: The principles and practices of 2D stop motion naturally translate to a 2D CGI environment.

# TECHNIQUES + STYLES

## TECHNIQUES

**HAND DRAWN**
Created with many materials (pencil, paint, ink, charcoal, etc.). Styles range from Disney cel to rotoscoping (tracing live action) to more fine art approach.

**2D STOP MOTION**
Made with a camera overhead a flat surface, created with many materials (sand, oil paint, paper silhouettes & cut-outs, photos). Light boxes used for sand, oil paint, paper silhouettes.

**3D STOP MOTION**
Made with a camera on a tripod, and created with many materials (puppets, models, clay, found objects, pixilation with human puppets).

**2D CGI**
Animation created in a flat or 2D software environment. Can be made entirely inside a program, or can be combined with traditional elements by scanning, coloring, laying out, or drawing directly into software.

**3D CGI**
Animation created in a 3D software environment. Elements are modeled, rigged, textured, puppeted, and animated in virtual space.

## STYLES

*consider for all techniques*

**FLUID TRANSITIONS**
Animation flows from one scene to the other seamlessly without cuts. Can appear to be morphing. Used for narrative storytelling that smoothly unwraps from beginning to end.

**2D/VECTOR/ KINETIC TYPE**
Flat design with highly scalable solid colors. Art comes from Illustrator and other vector programs. Often used for broadcast graphics, infographics, and Web design.

**HANDMADE**
Designs use real materials, often include texture, and look DIY. Hand drawn and stop motion are popular here. Used when trying to achieve a vintage or innocent feeling.

**COLLAGE**
Combines handmade elements with photos and video footage. Often used for animated documentary and title sequences.

**FILM & TYPE**
Combines video footage (often montaged) with kinetic type. Often used for non-linear title sequnces.

**3D**
Created with stop motion or CGI. "Real" light, shadows, and familiar gravity cues the audience to associate environment with reality.

3D stop motion utilizes a tripod to shoot incrementally moving objects on a "set." There's a huge range of objects that can be animated using 3D stop motion, including puppets, models, clay, found materials, and pixilation of human puppets. 3D stop motion can feel as naturalistic as CGI (see Henry Selick's *Coraline*) but can also maintain a quirky, handmade quality depending on the material used. "Found objects" can feel especially poetic when used in 3D stop motion and tend to have a humorous or metaphoric affect (see Jan Švankmajer and PES). Please note: The principles and practices of 3D stop motion naturally translate to a 3D CGI environment.

## 2D CGI

2D CGI is animation that is created in a flat or two-dimensional software environment. This technique is clean, is highly scalable, and reads well for type, which is why most broadcast graphics (print, Web, and TV) are done with 2D CGI animation. For narrative films, 2D CGI tends to feel warmer and more innocent than 3D, and its long history of use in children's programming has an emotionally "relatable" feeling. 2D CGI can be made in many software programs that use both bitmap and vector images.

## 3D CGI

3D CGI is animation that is made in a three-dimensional software environment. Elements are modeled, rigged, textured, puppeted, and animated in a virtual space. The process is similar to stop motion, with the key difference being that in 3D CGI there is no gravity and virtually no limitations. Because there are so many options, it can be the hardest technique to master and yet has some of the greatest rewards. 3D CGI allows you to create environments and characters that are almost indecipherable from real life. The immense power of 3D CGI to create hyper-realistic worlds makes it the technique of choice for special effects, video games, and many commercials.

# CONFORM OR ADAPT

Ideally the chart shown earlier helped you choose the right techniques and styles for your story, and you're off to the races. Once you've chosen, head to the Web and research examples of that technique/style in action. Seek inspiration in what others have done well, and decide if there is guidance you can glean from... *WAIT, what? You don't know that technique? And you've got no time to learn it??* No worries! You simply need to do the Darwinian thing: Adapt.

Say that after some soul-searching you recognize that a hand-drawn technique, specifically the ancient art of Chinese calligraphy, will work best for your project. That fluid, black brush stroke will sell your idea beautifully and nail your tone. And yet you have zero experience in hand-lettering and can barely find Asia on the map! Don't panic, you're simply on the road to finding an adaptation.

First thing to do is identify the defining characteristics of your desired technique. In the case of Chinese calligraphy, this is black brush strokes with a "liquid" quality. Now head back to the medium you're most comfortable with. Research tools, plug-ins, and tutorials to see if there's any way to achieve the desired effect within your favorite medium. Many programs will offer some kind of workaround that captures (at very least) some crucial element of your desired technique. With some luck, you'll find a near match. If you get very lucky (and stay flexible), you may even find a hybrid that both embodies what you're looking for and also aligns with your unique artistic point of view.

Karin Fong's *God of War III* title sequence is a great example of an adapted technique (at right). Fong and her amazing team at Imaginary Forces adapted 3D CGI animation to look and feel like flat illustrations on ancient Greek pottery. No small task, so let's take a look at her process.

# Case Study: Adapt 3D to Feel Like 2D

**Karin Fong**, Director, Title Sequence, *God of War III*.
Produced by Imaginary Forces and Sony PlayStation

Sony PlayStation's *God of War III* is a popular computer game that followed the lead of feature films by creating a stunning and complex main title sequence. The opening sequence brands the game as a dramatic epic informed by ancient history. The challenge for Karin Fong (director, designer, and founding member of Imaginary Forces) was in finding a balance between the game's modern 3D world and its ancient backstory. Says Fong, "The design of the titles and the sequences were meant to stand as flashbacks, through the lens of memory, and not be at all confused with the 'real-time' happenings of the current (3D) game."

Fong took inspiration from ancient Greek pottery as a way to relate to the story's roots in Greek mythology. She used Greek motifs in the borders, patterns, and ornaments, allowing for some strikingly graphic moments.

But her technique was even more striking. Through a long production pipeline, 2D and 3D animators worked together to find the right balance between the two techniques. They adapted the original 3D CGI models from the *GOW III* game, rendering and adding texture to achieve the graphic silhouettes that were more organic to Greek friezes. Says Fong, "We were very deliberate in finding a flat and graphic 2D influence to contrast with the look of the 3D game. It became a play between this extremely flat language and dimensional elements, with the hope that the tension between the two made for compelling imagery."

The result: animation and transitions that are startlingly elegant and classic but also modern and immediate. The sequence has a strange mix of dimensionality and flatness, a perfect mesh of 2D and 3D. Fong's adaptation came about by stretching the limits of the chosen technique to create the feel that was embodied in the message of the title sequence. Fong's thoughts guide and confirm how important it is to select the technique that best works for your story, and not the one you are most enamored with: "You need to know what message and emotion you want to convey first. Then you make sure the look is answering those questions. Don't be seduced by the technique, because it can really take away from the message of your project."

## Workarounds

If you did not find a satisfactory hybrid method within your program, then it's time to seek a workaround. This means getting a little DIY. Still-images, live-action footage, and (gasp) hiring help are all good moves. None of these options should feel daunting, and certainly should not feel like cheating. Instead, finding a good workaround is a sign of flexibility—successful industry professionals do it all the time, and Darwin would be proud.

### Workaround 1: Import still images

Perhaps the most common workaround in animation and motion graphics is to simply import still images and work with them inside your program. By using editing tools like masking (hiding and revealing parts of the image) and camera panning, you can get a still image "moving" in a way that almost feels like full-on animation. In the instance of our Chinese calligraphy, "unmasking" the lettering could even simulate the human quality of a real brushstroke executed by a human hand.

### Workaround 2: Shoot live-action footage

If still photos aren't cutting it, then live-action footage shot with a video camera is your next best alternative. Need to animate fire? Light a match and capture the images. Moving clouds? Tilt your lens up to the sky and get what you need. In the case of our Chinese calligraphy, you'll need to find someone to help out who can actually paint the brushstrokes. (FYI, you'd be surprised how far a social media post can take you in procuring that kind of talent.) Once you have your talent, set up your camera under good lighting and shoot close-up footage of the artist's brush as it creates the calligraphy. Once you've captured that footage, import it into your chosen program and composite it into your project. The sky is the limit for how you process and edit that footage once it's in, but the goal is to integrate your live action footage into the world of animated storytelling in a seamless way.

## Workaround 3: Staff up

Like it or not, you are the producer of your film, and being a producer means that if you can't get something done by yourself, *outsource it*. If you don't have the money to hire someone (which is often the case), favors, barter, and cajoling might get you what you need. Once you've secured the right talent, direct them closely, but leave some room for them to be creative, too. Oh, and coffee—you'll need to know their coffee order and have it ready when their energy drops. You'll be surprised at how much good work a simple non-fat latte and cinnamon scone will get you in a pinch!

## Case Study: Live Action and Hand Drawn

*Sensory Overload* directed by Miguel Jiron is an animated documentary created as part of an online media research project entitled "Interacting with Autism." The film is about a boy who struggles with autism spectrum disorder (ASD) and has a hard time processing a lot of sensory stimulation at once. It begins with simple documentary footage of a crowded city street. The color live-action footage cross dissolves into naturalistically drawn black-and-white animation of the boy on the street. With the switch from one technique to the other, the audience is cued that they're experiencing the film from the autistic boy's point of view. As the boy begins to struggle, the black-and-white drawing becomes layered with rings of vibrating watercolor. Realistic sounds of the city builds layer-by-layer into a cacophony of piercing agitated noises. The audience is taken to the uncomfortable place of experiencing the pain, confusion, and disorientation of sensory overload (at right).

The hand-drawn animation works to separate us from the boy as an individual person, but joins us with him as a character, and therefore is incredibly effective in creating empathy for the film's message. The splashes of watercolor are emotional and fluid and also metaphoric (the boy's emotions are being "flooded" by watercolors) and open the door for audiences to live in the intensity of the boy's perception. *Sensory Overload*'s elegant combination of documentary footage and drawn animation takes the audience on an unexpected journey of understanding and compassion.

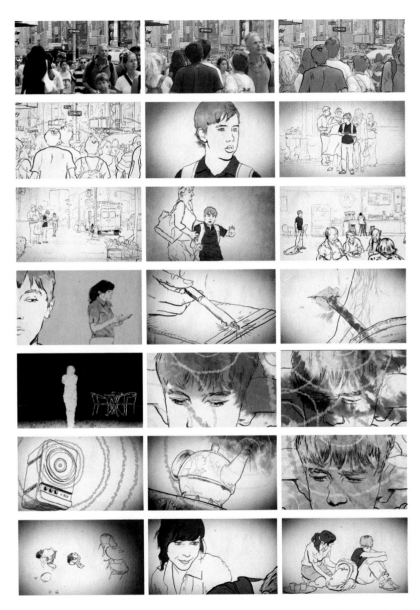

**Miguel Jiron**, *Sensory Overload: Interacting with Autism*. Produced and Directed by Mark Jonathan Harris, Marsha Kinder, and Scott Mahoy

## Case Study: 3D CGI

Director Maciek Janicki's masterfully animated short *Paper City* captures the rise and fall of a glorious city made completely of 3D CGI paper. As the artist describes on his website: "The narrative unfolds through winding roads, erupting forests and emerging mountains. In one fluid take, with skyscrapers rising from the page—only to crumble, wrinkle and gently crease back into the ground." While the story may sound simple, *Paper City* is packed with metaphors. While watching, audiences may ponder the impermanence of life, the transience of human civilization, and also the birth and death of paper as a medium since the advent of digital media (at right).

Inspired by traditional origami, Janicki used 3D CGI to model monochromatic paper to feel like a realistic yet magical world. Because the camera movement, lighting, and shadow are so organic and familiar, the audience is able to experience the film as a kind of recognizable space. *Paper City* takes advantage of 3D CGI's unique ability to morph reality with fantasy and gives us a front row seat to the birth and death of a city. Technique and story are in perfect sync, a match made in heaven. We experience the film for its story first, enjoying the layered meaning while savoring every frame of elegant animation.

### TECHNIQUE RECAP

1. Consider the Format
2. Translate Your Story
3. Consider Many Techniques
4. Consider Many Visual Styles
5. Adapt Your Technique
6. Workaround Using a New Technique
7. Import Still Images
8. Shoot Live-Action Footage
9. Staff Up

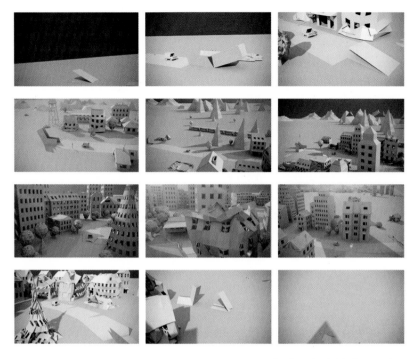

## ASSIGNMENT

Design a title sequence

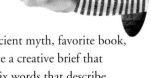

Design a one-minute title sequence inspired by an ancient myth, favorite book, or piece of music using the following process: 1. Write a creative brief that includes the title, target audience, and genre. 2. List six words that describe the "feeling" you would like your piece to have. 3. Jot down a list of images to trigger the key ideas that will define your sequence. 4. From the chart provided, choose the technique(s) that best fit the words and images you've listed. 5. Storyboard your sequence, select sound and/or music, and test two to three techniques that you think will best capture the feeling of your story. 6. Animate the title sequence.

# 9

# ANIMATE!

## Big-picture thinking, frame by frame

Congrats! You now have all the tools you could possibly need to create a masterfully animated story. You've constructed your storyboards, color script, and soundtrack—you've designed your world and selected a technique that expresses your big idea. You're off to the races, and animation should be easy breezy. And yet, in my experience, animation is exactly the step when all hell can break loose. The reason is simple: Each of your carefully constructed elements—magical on their own—can be stubborn when united and put into motion. Though you may have envisioned yourself in an elegant concert hall conducting a disciplined symphony orchestra, you may find yourself in a dank basement filled with feral cats, and you're in charge of trimming their nails. It can feel overwhelming...

Never fear! Your project will work just as planned. You only need to follow a few insider tips that will keep you centered and moving forward towards your goal. The following wisdom was born of generations of tough-as-nails animators who experienced failure, heartbreak, and humiliation, only to rise up like the Phoenix and live to tell their tale. So pay your respects, and pay close attention.

# GET STARTED

The obvious way to go about animating your project is to start at the beginning, but that's not necessarily the best way to go. You need to build up your confidence, get used to uniting your elements, and become accustomed to the unique (and sometimes infuriating) eccentricities of the medium.

## Start Easy, Gain Confidence

I encourage you to start by animating your project's "low-hanging fruit," that is, the most fun, short, and easy-to-animate scene. Approaching your easiest sequences first will get you moving forward and most importantly will help build up your confidence at a time when you may be feeling insecure. Once you're done animating that first "easy" scene, head to the next one that you think is especially do-able, even if it's not the next one in your sequence. Done with that? Start on the next. After completing a few of those simpler sequences, you'll be far better equipped to tackle the tough ones… *and by then you'll have no choice!*

## Break Up the Tough Ones

When you do arrive at your more challenging scenes, don't try to tackle them in one go. You're not David battling Goliath, and this ain't Biblical times. Your best bet in animating a tough sequence is to break it up into smaller pieces that are easier to handle, and then work on those pieces one by one. Not only will breaking it up make the tough scene less intimidating, it will also reinforce the important notion that animated sequences are often mini-story arcs with distinct beginnings, middles, and ends. Take the launch of a spaceship: Far from just a simple "launch," it includes the gathering up of energy, forward momentum brought on by fire, and finally the lift-off. The big launch, like

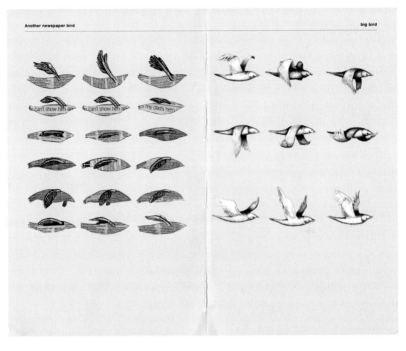

**Maciek Janicki**, *Interim Flight*

many of your animated sequences, is its own story arc, and working on it in parts not only will make it less daunting but will strengthen your storytelling as well.

## No Shot Left Behind

It doesn't take an industry veteran to tell you that animation takes a long time. The process is so labor intensive that a 12-hour day could pass with little more completed than a 3-second shot. The snail's pace can be enough to make you pull your hair out. To avoid putting yourself through the torture of animating what is not absolutely necessary, you must become a brutal editor. I'm talking Genghis Khan, Attila the Hun brutal. Before commencing work on a sequence of animation, ask yourself sternly if the shot is absolutely worth it story-wise. If not, guillotine-time. And if you're reluctant to edit the sequence because it's

**Ariel Costa,** *Welcome to the Aescripts + Aeplugins Playground*

your "coolest part," then *definitely* consider cutting it. Because it's usually the *look-what-I-can-do!* shots that hold back your story and add unnecessary time to your production schedule. Wanna show off? Tell your friends you finished your project early and that you're headed to the beach!

## Protect Ya' Tech

This is a book about storytelling, but there will be no stories told if you lose it all to a crash or technical error. Save versions early and often. When you're naming things, think best practices: Create simple filenames and folders that are logical and organized. You're never going to find that version you called "need_sleep_finalfinal.pdf" no matter how hard you look. Disorganization has derailed more productions than computer crashes so heed this advice. Finally, get yourself the biggest blank hard drive you can afford and back up your work at the end of every day. Hell, triple-back it up. Don't be the fool who has to learn this lesson the hard way when so many others have already learned it for you.

# STRATEGIC MOVEMENT

Sure, we spent a whole chapter on storyboards and yours are good enough to hang in a museum. But in the animated realm things change, so roughing out your sequences in a more elaborate way is essential.

## Be a Poser

Called *key poses*, these more elaborate sketches (which are best accomplished in your medium of choice or program of choice) provide a guide to ensure that all of your planned movement is possible, that you hit your intended marks of choreography, and that all of your assets conform to the world you've created. When creating your key poses, don't forget to include all elements—your backgrounds, props, and even text and logos that you intend to have occupy the screen. You'd be surprised how many experienced animators have painstakingly walked a character across a room only to realize later that they've walked them through a table!

## Anticipate and Follow Through

When working on your key poses, don't forget to pay homage to the Patron Saints of animation: Anticipation and Follow Through. These "before and after" movements help illustrate the physics of gravity on weight and movement. Anticipation and follow through are as important as your "main" movements and are responsible for making your animation feel natural. A woman running to catch a bus doesn't simply start pumping her arms and legs. Her body first leans back to gather momentum for the run. And then when she stops at the bus, her hair and dress swing forward as a result of the gathered force of motion. Everything that moves in your film, whether it be a character, shape, logo, or piece of text, requires anticipation and follow though. Without it, your movement will feel robotic and flat, and your audience will sense that the same is true of your story.

## Compose Directional Movement

Unlike in the real world, objects on a screen are two-dimensional. Even though it may seem as though they have depth, the track of on-screen movement is always flat. As a result, all animated objects move along an invisible directional path that falls into four simple categories: horizontal, vertical, diagonal, and circular. It's important to be mindful of the directional movement of all objects in your sequences as it can enhance (or detract from) the emotional experience of your piece. Movement that is directionally consistent (all vertical and horizontal, for instance) will feel calmer and so is best used for scenes meant to give the audience a sense of ease. But if you want to adjust the emotional environment (say a villain enters), then adding a movement that contrasts to the predominant direction can clue the audience into a big story moment.

### PATH FOR DIRECTIONAL MOVEMENT

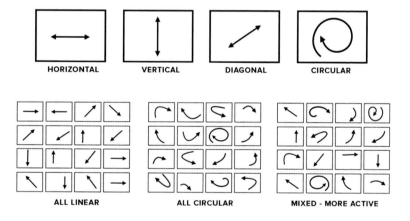

Two baby mice walk peacefully in the forest and move only along vertical and horizontal linear paths—but when an evil fox enters, he moves on a diagonal or even circular path. In a scene meant to be intense and jarring (say the fox pounces on the mice), using multiple directions from shot to shot will intensify the visual drama and unsettle the audience, alerting them to menace.

Before animating, chart the path of your film's directional movement by printing out your storyboards (or key pose sketches) and drawing simple lines on each to show the general path that your objects are following. Consider how you can enhance the story you're telling with the directions you compose.

## Decentralize and Mix It Up

Since you've already got your storyboards out, I want you to double-check that your shots are as interesting as they can be by conceding to a few of the fundamentals of visual filmmaking.

### Fundamental 1: Get out of the center

Don't plop your subject in the center of your frame (too often). I know, we talked about this in Chapter 3, but this is your last chance to make good. Take the time to check that there aren't too many compositions with the subject, logo, or type in the center of the frame. Mix it up or risk having visually sleep-inducing sequences in your film. If you really need your subject dead center, consider starting with it somewhere else first and then moving it towards the center. Decentralizing your subject will keep your shots active and exciting.

### Fundamental 2: Mix up shot length

Don't forget to mix up your shot lengths. Much like with centering, too many shots with similar shot lengths will bore your viewer. Notice when you're watching well-directed films how in one sequence the frame cuts from long shots to medium shots and then to close ups? The eye likes to experience a variety of focal lengths and to follow the visual cues set by the amount of information in the frame.

Mixing up the scale of your subject inside the frame and the amount of information you include in the frame enhances the experience of your story. A beetle is having an anxiety attack but manages to calm herself before walking on-stage to deliver a speech. A medium-wide shot for the whole sequence would not only be a snoozer but a missed opportunity. You need to use the visual story to squeeze out all of the emotion you can get from the scene. A moment of great anxiety (or claustrophobia) can be enriched with a close-up, even an extreme close-up. But you don't want to stay close too long. Once the beetle gathers her composure, you might shift to a medium shot. Then your frame might widen, continuing so until finally widening to a long shot when the beetle walks on-stage completely self-assured. Mixing up your shot lengths not only will keep your sequences visually varied and interesting but most importantly will help communicate the big ideas in your story.

### Fundamental 3: Mix up shot timing

In addition to varying the size of your shots, vary the timing of your shots so that your sequences move at different paces. Some shots may work at a full 15 seconds before cutting, while others need cutting at just 2 or 3 seconds. Varying your timing will offer a less predictable visual experience for your audience. Many filmmakers use quicker shots for more frantic scenes and longer ones for calmer scenes—some filmmakers do the opposite. But *successful* filmmakers always mix 'em up for best effect.

## Consider the Blur

When shooting film or video, the camera's lens has a limited ability to focus on objects at different focal lengths. The optics of lenses create lovely images that are both sharp in some areas and blurry in others. Light traveling though the lens creates a uneven exposure resulting in a vignette or darkening around the edges. When animating in computer software, however, everything is in focus all the time and the "exposure" is uniform. This "super-clean" sharpness can be harsh and lack focal points. It's up to you to add some variation by considering where to add a blur effect and other such shot-enhancing devices as *grain, grunge,* or *vignette.* These can help add realistic depth to shots that might otherwise feel flat and uninteresting and can also help de-emphasize areas of your composition that aren't important to the emotion of the scene. Whether you seek something realistic or more stylized, a slight blur or darkening of the corners (or addition of the effects listed above) will help bring your piece to the next level.

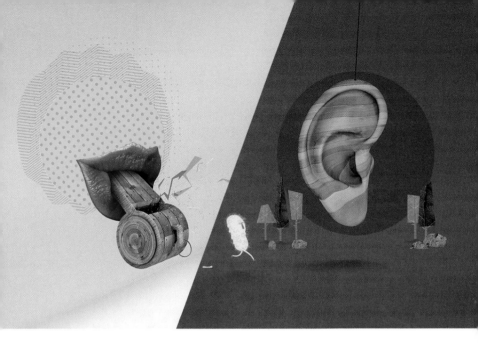

**Ariel Costa**, *Feed Your Creative Brain*, State Design, Motion Conference

## SOUND IT OUT

You've probably figured out by now that story can evolve as your production moves towards completion. Luckily, everything is malleable in animated production, and sound is no exception. So while you may believe that your soundtrack is locked or that you've found the perfect opening song for your film, a mere tweak in story may require a new sound treatment throughout. Modifying sound after you thought you had it right may make you uneasy, especially once you've become accustomed to the sound you've painstakingly chosen—but the result will be worth it. Stay flexible and don't stop tweaking until sound fits the story you want to tell.

The process of tweaking your sound during production will also train you to work on sound and image simultaneously as things develop. Take that lesson to heart. It will force you (again) to consider the great power of sound to affect emotional flow and to elevate your story until it matches your vision.

## Be Flexible with Soundtrack

As your piece evolves, the music and effects that felt right in pre-production may not be the best choice for the final animation. Be open to change, and expect to spend some time experimenting. Sometimes this process will affirm your original sound was the right choice, and sometimes it will reveal that your work can reach a new level, paired with a different tone or tempo. You can always pop in multiple soundtracks and render to see how it works. Nothing helps to give you fresh perspective on a project more than a shift in music and effects, so if your current soundtrack isn't working, use it as an opportunity and dig deeper.

## Hit Your Sound Marks

Now that you've chosen your "temp" music (I call it temp because music can always change) and you have your effects and any dialogue, it's essential that you animate to your soundtrack. Animators often refer to the choreography of a sequence. This is because animation is a kind of dance, a back and forth between sound and image that is rhythmically paced and elegantly timed. Allow your soundtrack to influence your sequences and augment storytelling opportunities.

## Mute Your Soundtrack

On the other hand, be careful that your sound isn't doing all the work! Sound effects, music, and dialogue (your soundtrack) can be so powerful that an animator can unintentionally rely on it too heavily and not give a strong enough animated performance. Press mute now and again to see how your shots are playing with no sound at all. If your visuals lack the expressiveness to be compelling on their own, you may be depending too much on your soundtrack. This is especially important for character animation with dialogue. A great voice track can make you think that a great performance is coming from the animation. Turn off the sound and see if your character's face and body are doing the acting or if it's just the voice.

# ANIMATE! RECAP

1. Easy shots first to gain confidence
2. Break up tough shots into pieces
3. Plan well so no animation is cut
4. Back up your digital files
5. Pose your shots before animating
6. Movement tip: Always anticipate and follow through
7. Compose directional movement for whole film

8. Compose shots so subject isn't always in the center
9. Mix up shot length throughout film
10. Mix up shot timing throughout film
11. Add blur and vignettes
12. Be flexible with soundtrack
13. Listen to sound while animating to hit sound marks
14. Mute your soundtrack to check movement

## ASSIGNMENT
Create a short with a message

Animate a 60 second (or less) short with a message that is important to you. Your subject can have a social, political, or moral meaning or can simply express an opinion that you feel would make an interesting film. Try using voiceover or text to communicate your idea. Go through the recaps in this book to remind yourself of the steps you need to take to create a meaningful animated story. You are an animated storyteller now, with the tools to create something magical, so get cracking!

# 10

## SHOW AND TELL
### Create, share, and network

More than any other time in history, you now have the opportunity to make your work seen. Film festivals have proliferated, the Internet has opened countless forums to celebrate new work, and sharing content has become so embedded in our culture that your little animated project could go from your laptop to being a global sensation in minutes. Quite suddenly, every animated story has the potential to become a hit, viewed not only by the masses but by important industry folks looking for fresh talent. At the same time, the market is flooded with content. Cable networks are battling digital players such as Netflix, Amazon, and Hulu, not to mention more than 500 million YouTube channels. Sure, there are more film festivals now, but the high-profile ones are more competitive than ever. Sundance alone receives more than 9,000 submissions a year for roughly 200 spots.

# GET IT OUT THERE

So how does an animated storyteller with a completed project (like you) find an audience? How can your work distinguish itself from the crowd? It's all in these final steps of *Animated Storytelling*, aimed at getting your project seen not only by the most eyeballs but the right eyeballs. You've told a powerful story in your film; now it's time for you to tell the story *of* your film.

## Step 1: Package Your Project

The first step in packaging your project is all about design. Until very recently this meant creating a DVD and informational one-sheet and then heading to the post office. Today almost everything is submitted online, so you'll need to create a working link (password protected for festivals) that's ready to share. But whether you're making DVDs or not, you'll still need to create the following physical assets:

*Title Logo and Still:* Design a clean, quickly legible logo for the title of your project paired with a still "photo" from your film that embodies the story. The logo and still are necessary for promotional materials and can be displayed on your website, as a cover for DVDs, or on posters for film festivals.

*Synopsis:* Write a tight, clear description of your project, two to three sentences tops. This description will be quoted (likely verbatim) on websites and other publications well into the future, so get it right.

*Director Bio:* Start your bio with what you want to be known as professionally (such as animation director or screenwriter), and then follow it up with your accomplishments that support that role. If you're just starting out, then list an interesting fact about yourself or some background that people might find interesting. Some animators like to write quirky bios, and if you go that way just make sure it pertains directly to the content of your project. For example, if you've made a film about bats, you might say, "Kelly Dunn is an animator from Texas. At night she sleeps hanging upside down from the ceiling."

***Story of the Film:*** Finally, you'll need to have the story of your film's creation written out and memorized for future interviews. This story begins with why you wanted to make your film in the first place and why there is such a need to tell your story. This can be highly personal or related to a broad issue that you wanted to explore. For example, my animated documentary film *Backseat Bingo* explored the romantic lives of seniors. I was inspired by watching my grandfather Sid fall in love at 84 years old, and I wanted to portray seniors in a way that I felt the media was missing: as smart, funny, and still surprisingly lustful…just like my grandpa Sid.

## Step 2: Creating Your Network
### Networking, online version:

If you aren't already an active participant in the plethora of online communities for designers, filmmakers, and artists sharing their work and ideas online, then get on it. The Internet provides the chance to connect with amazing people all over the world. Real relationships can form and lead to big opportunities so long as you cultivate those contacts with professionalism and respect. Between Facebook and Vimeo groups, AWN, *Animation Magazine*, *Motiongrapher*, Cartoon Brew, ASIFA, AIGA, and, of course, Tumblr, Behance, and Instagram (and whatever new container is invented by the time this book is printed), go get active. Find your peers and make friends. Seek out groups of like-minded artists and also groups that share a common thread with the story of your film. For *Backseat Bingo*, that meant animators and documentarians but also senior citizen groups that I thought would be interested in my work.

Once you join an online community, be present and engaged. Blog, post, share links that you find interesting, and make connections. When you're established there and feel ready to share your project, *do not give it all away*. Tease it out with character designs, sketches, articles of interest that connect to your film's theme. Pique your online network's interest so that they come asking to see your work instead of you having to nudge.

**Julia Pott**, *Triangle*

Networking, human version:

Let me guess, you find socializing at industry events to be a special kind of torture, and the idea of "networking" makes you want to stick your head in a hole? Guess what? You're not alone. I'm a bit of a goof and get insecure at conferences and festivals. However, when I agreed to write this book I realized that I'd better get over it, especially since I knew I needed to meet some awesome people who would agree to contribute illustrations. As mentioned, I'm kinda quirky, but instead of trying to become someone I'm not, I leaned into my inner goof and it's worked wonders…

144    Animated Storytelling

Exhibit A: I attended the F5 conference in NYC and there standing 10 feet away, engaged in a conversation, was my hero, director/animator/illustrator Julia Pott. I noticed others waiting to talk to her, too. So I did something straight-up rid-onk-ulous. I stood behind the person Ms. Pott was conversing with, put my hands into a heart shape, and danced around, hoping that she would embrace my silly gesture of admiration. Her face lit up. She said, "Hello!" I said, "I love you." She said, "How about a hug?" I told her that her work was incredibly inspiring and mentioned that I was writing this book. I followed up with a short email and asked Julia to contribute an illustration to my book. The result is to the left, a drawing of her friends called *Triangle*. I adore it, especially since in my own wacky way, I did just that: I entered one of my hero's Triangles. And so can you.

## Share and Repeat

The time has come. You've fully packaged your completed film and are ready to share it. Who you send it to depends solely on the dream in your heart. Only advice here is to be as professional as humanly possible. If you want your project seen by film festival audiences worldwide, learn about which festivals are the best fit for your film, read the submission guidelines, and get everything in on time.

If you're trying to get hired, craft your correspondences in a way that reflects your capacity as a professional. Employers appreciate artistic talent, but even more they want to hire someone who is dependable and articulate—they want someone who can get the work done easier and faster. At the very least, spell-check *everything*.

And one more thing: Never stop. Being an artist is a constant itch. After completing this project you may need a day's rest, but as soon as you feel that itch to create again, yield to it. Sketch, storyboard, write, animate, dream, and experiment your way to new, amazing stories. And stay in touch. Ask me questions or share your work in my Facebook group Animated Storytelling or find me at www.lizblazer.com. You can count me in as part of your network, and I'll be rooting for your stories to come alive.

# A LITTLE EXTRA INSPIRATION

What we need is more people who
specialize in the impossible. - Theodore Roethke

I believe in the truth of fairy-tales more than
I believe in the truth in the newspaper. - Lotte Reiniger

I love Mickey Mouse more than any
woman I have ever known. - Walt Disney

After nourishment, shelter and companionship, stories
are the thing we need most in the world. - Philip Pullman

Great stories happen to those who can tell them. - Ira Glass

A story should have a beginning, a middle and an end...
but not necessarily in that order. - Jean-Luc Godard

The number one barrier to creativity
is a clearly defined goal. - Chris Do

We have to continually be jumping off cliffs and
developing our wings on the way down. - Kurt Vonnegut

Everything stinks till it's finished. - Dr. Seuss

To invent, you need a good imagination
and a pile of junk. - Thomas Edison

Telling yourself you have all the time in the world,
all the money in the world, all the colors in the palette,
anything you want - that just kills creativity. - Jack White

In an animated film you can do whatever you want,
but that doesn't mean you should do everything you want.
- John Lasseter

Never mistake motion for action. - Ernest Hemingway

Work? It's just serious play. - Saul Bass

# START YOUR NEXT FILM HERE!

# INDEX

surprise or unexpected use of, 67
symbolism related to, 60
thematic and accent, 66
tips for using, 63–69
*Color Blind* (Borst), 24–25
color scripts, 58–62
  examples of, 56, 59, 61
  pre-color scripts and, 58–61
  principal colors in, 60, 62
  process of completing, 62
  supporting colors in, 61, 62
comfort zone, going beyond, 74–75
coming of age stories, 35
complementary colors, 64
composing shots, 43–44
concept art, 9
concept development, 2–9
  creative brief in, 2–4
  honing your pitch in, 7–9
  summoning the muse in, 4–7
continuity, 48–49
  directional, 49
  issues with, 102
  spatial, 48–49
  temporal, 49
contrasting music, 94
Costa, Ariel, viii, 16, 36, 54, 66, 70, 86,
  100, 112, 128, 132, 137, 140
countdown story structure, 29
creative brief, 2–4, 116
cue cards, 18–19
Cytowic, Richard E., 97

**D**

*Daily Monsters Project* (Bucher), 78, 79
dead zones, 46
decentralizing subjects, 135
dialogue, 95–96
diegetic sound, 89–90
directional continuity, 49
directional movement, 134–135
director bio, 142
Disney, Walt, 37–38
drawing style, 42
Dulaney, Kim, 63, 64, 68, 108, 109
dynamic framing, 44

**E**

editing your work, 131–132
effects added to shots, 136
elevator pitch, 8
emotions and music, 93
ending your story, 22–23
*Eno* (Dulaney), 64
environmental design, 102–108
  assignment on, 110–111
  physical laws in, 104–105
  social laws in, 106–107
  time and place in, 103–104
  visual laws in, 107–108
experimentation, 11–12, 71–85
  applying to current projects, 80–83
  assignment utilizing, 85
  creating "bad" art through, 73
  expanding your skill set with, 74–75
  with movement, 82–83
  with non-digital sources, 85
  with personal projects, 79
  with sound, 99
  with transitions, 80–81
  with work you want to be hired for,
    76–79
*Exquisite Corpse* (Waldron), 32–33

**F**

failing better, 74, 75
*Feed Your Creative Brain* (Costa), 137
*Feed Your Creative Brain* (Scirocco), 83
file management, 132
film & type style, 118
"first love" story, 5–6, 8–9
fluid transitions, 80–81, 118
Foley sound effects, 92
follow through, 133
Fong, Karin, 89, 120–122
framing process, 44–45, 135

**G**

Gilliam, Terry, 117
Glitschka, Von, 67
*God of War III* title sequence, 120–122
good vs. evil stories, 35

**31901056707989**